ELVIS

ELVIS

timothy frew

MALLARD PRESS

An Imprint of BDD Promotional Book Company, Inc.
666 Fifth Avenue
New York, NY 10103

A FRIEDMAN GROUP BOOK

Published by MALLARD PRESS
An Imprint of BDD Promotional Book Company, Inc.
666 Fifth Avenue
New York, N.Y. 10103

Mallard Press and its accompanying design and logo are trademarks of BDD Promotional
Book Company, Inc.

ISBN 0-7924-5754-4

ELVIS
was prepared and produced by
Michael Friedman Publishing Group, Inc.
15 West 26th Street
New York, New York 10010

Editor: Sharyn Rosart
Art Director: Jeff Batzli
Designer: Lynne Yeamans
Photography Editor: Daniella Jo Nilva

Typeset by Bookworks Plus
Color separations by Colourmatch Pte. Ltd.
Printed and bound in Hong Kong by Leefung-Asco Printers Ltd.

Dedication

To my brothers and sister, Dave, Doug, and Shelley. I love you all.

Acknowledgments

I would like to thank the people who have helped me work on this book: Sharyn Rosart, my editor, Lynne Yeamans, who did a wonderful job designing the book, and Daniella Jo Nilva, who is responsible for locating all the photographs. I would also like to acknowledge Ward Sanders, Mrs. Wiener, the Peabody Ducks, and Dick Vermeil, who all did their part in turning a simple trip to Graceland into a near-religious experience.

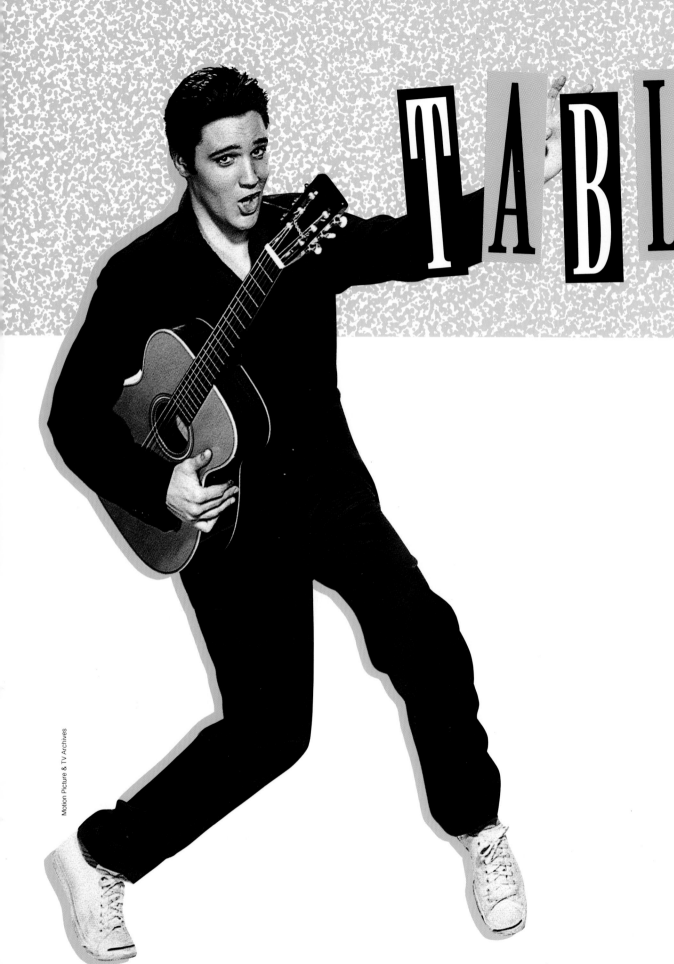

Motion Picture & TV Archives

TABLE of

CONTENTS

Michael Ochs Archive

Archive Photos

"Before Elvis there was nothing....Nothing
really affected me until Elvis."
—John Lennon

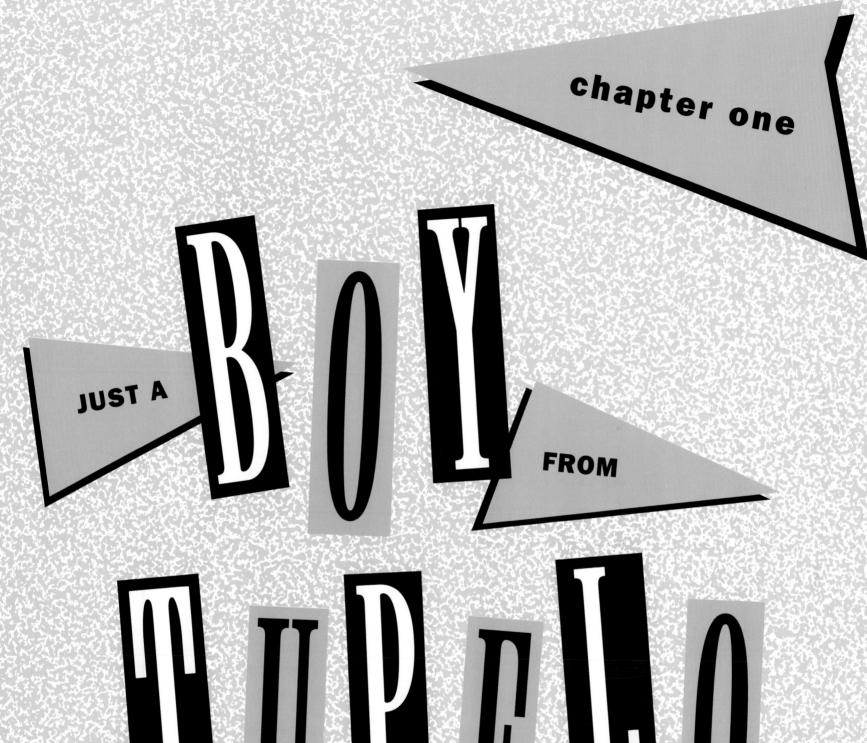

chapter one

JUST A BOY FROM TUPELO

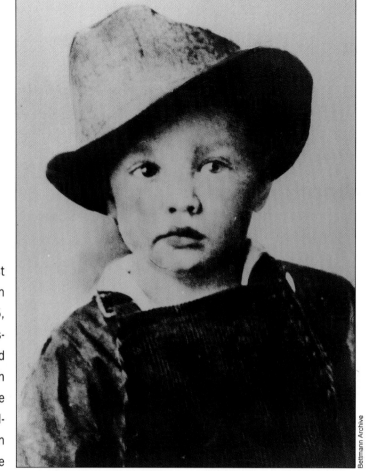

Bettmann Archive

In the hours just before dawn on January 8, 1935, in Tupelo, Mississippi, 23-year-old Gladys Love Smith Presley lay in the throes of childbirth. Frigid winds and rain pounded the thin walls of the thirty-by-fifteen-foot (9 x 4.5m) shotgun shack in which Gladys's husband, Vernon, and a local doctor kept a vigil over the young woman's progress. It had been a long, hard labor for Gladys, who was weak and delirious from the pain and lack of sleep. At 4:00 a.m., her first child, Jesse Garon Presley, was born. To the dismay of Vernon and Gladys, the baby was born dead. As Vernon and the doctor placed the dead infant in a small cardboard box, Gladys remained in labor. Much to everybody's surprise, a second child was on its way. Thirty-five minutes later, Elvis Aron Presley was born. The new parents' initial joy at the birth of Elvis was quickly overshadowed by the grief and despair caused by the loss of his twin brother. An hysterical Gladys desperately clung to her surviving child, not letting anyone near him for fear that he, too, would die. Finally, as Vernon attempted to console the new mother, the doctor managed to pry Elvis away from Gladys long enough to clean him off and wrap him in a blanket.

Jesse Garon was buried the next day in an unmarked grave in the Priceville Cemetery in Tupelo. Only Vernon, Gladys, the infant Elvis, and the minister were present at the funeral. Gladys refused to allow even her family and closest friends to come to the funeral to pay their respects, wishing instead to grieve in private. Today, the exact location of Jesse Garon's grave is unknown. In later years, Elvis wanted to return and put a marker on his twin brother's grave, but by that time, Gladys was dead and Vernon could not remember exactly where the grave was.

To say that Elvis's birth was inauspicious is an extreme understatement. The Presleys were dirt poor, even by the low standards of the small, Southern, Depression-era community of Tupelo, Mississippi. Considered one step above "white trash" by many of the residents of Tupelo, the Presleys were just slightly better off than the blacks of the area, if only by virtue of their skin color. The house at 306 Old Saltillo Road, in which Elvis was born, was built by his father about a year earlier with $180 worth of cheap lumber. (The house, which is still standing, was declared a state historical site by the Mississippi Department of Archives on January 8, 1977, Elvis's birthday, just seven months before his death. The address is now listed as 306 Elvis Presley Drive.)

With only an eighth-grade education, Vernon was an unambitious man who had difficulty holding onto a job. Those who knew Vernon considered him the king of the odd job. He would take work only when it was absolutely necessary, and would quit

Wide World Photos

before long, complaining of a bad back. He worked as a share-cropper, handyman, factory worker, truck driver, builder of out-houses, virtually any job that would give him a little money but could be quickly and easily abandoned once he grew tired of it.

Gladys, on the other hand, was a very proud, determined woman who clearly dominated every aspect of the Presley house-hold. She was constantly trying to make life better for her family. It was she who pushed Vernon into taking the few meager jobs he worked. Gladys herself took work as a sewing-machine operator and a cleaning lady, as well as many other odd jobs, in order to make ends meet.

Unable to have any more children, Gladys smothered Elvis with love. She was an extremely protective mother, who very seldom let the young Elvis out of her sight. In fact, Gladys used to walk

Elvis to school every day until he was fifteen, when the young teenager complained of being harassed by the other kids for being a "mama's boy." Gladys used to tell Elvis that his twin brother, Jesse Garon, was up in heaven looking over him to make sure nothing bad happened to him, and that she had to love Elvis twice as much because her other son had died. Growing up and throughout his life, Elvis would be obsessed with the idea that he had an identical twin. He would talk of and to Jesse as if he was still alive. Elvis truly believed, as his mother had taught him, that Jesse was up in heaven looking over him.

Born in Pontotoc, Mississippi, on April 25, 1912, Gladys Love Smith was the daughter of Robert Lee Smith and Octavia Luvenia Mansell Smith—otherwise known as "Doll". Gladys was the fifth of nine children: Effie (1904), Lillian, (1906), Levalle (1908), Travis

This two-room frame home is the birthplace of Elvis Presley. The house was built by Vernon Presley with $180 worth of lumber. Elvis lived in this house for the first five years of his life.

Archive Photos

Many people close to the Presleys maintain that once Elvis was born and Jesse died, things were never quite the same between Gladys and Vernon. Gladys channelled the grief she felt for the loss of one son into her love for the other. From the time Elvis was born until the day Gladys died, her entire life was devoted to her only son. She became very critical of Vernon's lack of ambition and faulted him for not being able to provide a better life for Elvis. Yet despite the tensions and perhaps loss of love between them, Gladys and Vernon remained together, essentially devoted to each other until Gladys's death in 1958. The family dynamic, however, was an odd, dysfunctional one. It was always Gladys and Elvis, mother and son, with Vernon on the outside, which is perhaps the way he wanted it.

Elvis was an attractive, if slightly awkward, youth. He had a fair complexion with blond hair and huge blue eyes. Always a bit of a loner, Elvis had very few friends as a child. He spent most of his time with his mother.

Like most families living in the South at the time, the Presleys were a God-fearing family that went to church every Sunday at the local Pentecostal church, the First Assembly of God. It was there, at a very young age, that Elvis had his first exposure to music. In his book, *The Boy Who Would Be King,* Elvis's second cousin, childhood friend, and eventual publicist, Earl Greenwood, recalls Gladys talking about Elvis's early love for music: "I remember taking Elvis to church, and even when he was an infant, he'd squirm in my lap whenever the singin' would start.... He tried singin' before he could even talk."

According to Gladys, when Elvis was about three years old, he used to sit contentedly on her lap during church until the music started. As soon as the choir would start up, however, Elvis would jump off his mother's lap and start running up and down the church aisle, dancing and singing along with the hymns, mimicking the words as best he could.

Music, especially gospel music, was an integral part of Southern culture at the time. In addition to the White gospel music he heard in church every week, Elvis was exposed to many other musical influences abundant in the South at the time. On the radio he heard country western, swing, and crooning pop music. From Tupelo's Black population, Elvis heard rhythm and blues as well as Black gospel. According to legend, Elvis used to go to the Black part of town on Sunday afternoons to sit outside the church and listen to the singing.

(1915), Tracy (1916), Clettes (1919), and John (1922). Gladys and her family moved to Tupelo from nearby West Point in the spring of 1933. It was there that she met the handsome, if uneducated, Vernon Elvis Presley, at the Assembly of God Church. The two quickly began dating and eloped just a few months later, after Vernon's seventeenth birthday. Gladys, who was four years Vernon's senior, would constantly lie about her age so as not to appear to be a cradle snatcher. In fact, because she lied about her age, many people believed Gladys to be forty-two when she died, when in fact, she was forty-six.

It is from all of these influences that Elvis developed his love for music as well as the unique singing and musical style that would later make him the most popular entertainer in the world. When reminiscing about his early exposure to music, Elvis always pointed to gospel as his main musical drive. In his 1968 comeback television special, Elvis declared, "Rock and roll is basically just gospel music, or gospel music mixed with rhythm and blues."

Elvis's favorite gospel groups were the quartets. He would later credit Jake Hess, the lead singer for the Statesman Quartet, as providing his greatest musical inspiration. Elvis used what he learned from such quartets as The Jordanaires, J.D. Sumner and the Stamps, and The Sweet Inspirations in his music throughout his career. More than anything, Elvis loved the sound of harmony. Later, he was often to complain that the engineers at RCA records mixed his vocals too loud, thus drowning out the sound of the background harmonies.

Even Elvis's lively stage persona and infamous hip swinging was based on what he saw in church. "We used to go to these religious singin's all the time," Elvis once stated in an interview. "There were these singers, perfectly fine singers, but nobody responded to them. Then there was the preachers and they cut up all over the place, jumpin' on the piano, movin' ever' which way. The audience liked 'em. I guess I learned from them."

One day, when he was a fifth grader at Lawhon Elementary School in East Tupelo, Elvis began singing the classic Red Foley country ballad "Old Shep" in class. His teacher, Mrs. Oleta Grimes, was so taken by Elvis's beautiful singing voice that she talked to the school's principal, J.D. Cole, about entering Elvis in the annual talent contest at the Mississippi-Alabama Fair and Dairy Show. In his first-ever public performance on October 3, 1945, Elvis Presley sang "Old Shep," unaccompanied by any instruments. The ten-year-old Presley was so short that he had to stand on a chair while he sang in order to reach the microphone. The Fair and Dairy Show was broadcast live on WELO radio in Tupelo, so it can be said that this was the future King's first-ever radio broadcast as well. Elvis won second prize—five dollars and free admission to all of the amusement rides. First prize went to Shirley Jones Gallentine, who sang "My Dreams Are Getting Better All the Time" and won a $25 war bond.

On January 8, 1946, for his eleventh birthday, Gladys bought Elvis his first guitar for $7.75. He originally wanted a bicycle; however, Gladys convinced him into taking the much cheaper guitar. According to Forrest L. Bobo, the proprietor of the Tupelo Hardware Company where Gladys bought the guitar, Elvis was looking at the guitar when he noticed a .22 caliber rifle for sale. Elvis whined and complained in a desperate attempt to convince his mother to buy him the gun instead of the guitar or the bicycle. As protective a mother as Gladys was, she would have nothing to do with guns. When Elvis was older, however, he became a gun enthusiast and an obsessive collector.

Elvis learned how to play a few chords from his two uncles, and then taught himself more of the basics by listening to the popular songs of the day and figuring them out on the fret board.

In the late summer of 1948, things suddenly got worse for the already downtrodden Presley family. Vernon was arrested for selling moonshine whiskey. While moonshine was a very popular commodity in the South in 1948, selling it was still a jailable offense. Ten years earlier, Vernon had spent eight months of a

Archive Photos

A young Elvis Presley already greasing his hair back. The slicked back hair and knowing sneer would soon be an Elvis Presley trademark.

ELVIS PRESLEY'S *All American City* TUPELO BIRTH PLACE MISSISSIPPI three-year sentence in Parchman Penitentiary for forging a check. The only reason he got out of that sentence early was because his family was destitute. This time, rather than sending Vernon back to jail, which would cause even further hardships on his family, the local authorities decided to drop the charges if Vernon agreed to leave the Tupelo area within two weeks.

"We were broke, man, broke, and we left Tupelo overnight," Elvis later recalled in an interview. "Dad packed all our belongings in boxes and put them on the top and in the trunk of a 1939 Plymouth. We headed for Memphis."

The culture shock for Elvis and the rest of the Presley clan must have been immense. Without much planning, the Presleys moved from a small rural town with a population of about 6,000 people to a booming Southern city of more than 300,000. Vernon saw the move as an opportunity to start over and become something better. Gladys, who was truly a country girl at heart, simply viewed the move with wary trepidation. One can only speculate on how Elvis felt. In an instant, he went from being a poor rural youth, where at least he had a few friends and knew what was expected of him, to being a poor urban kid—one face in thousands facing an entirely new set of cultural rules.

Despite the move and their hope of finding more and better jobs, things did not get any better for the Presleys. Vernon still had trouble finding and keeping work. They moved into the poorest White section of Memphis, and now didn't even have a house of their own. Their first Memphis home was a single room in a large boxlike house, where they had to share a kitchen and a bathroom with three other families. Vernon got a job working for a tool company, while Gladys worked as a waitress and a seamstress in a curtain factory. The combined Presley income during the family's first year in Memphis came to $35 a week, or $1,820 for the entire year.

Elvis enrolled in Humes High School in 1949. Already a loner, Elvis withdrew even further into himself. He felt like a poor rural "cracker" who didn't seem to fit in this new urban environment. While at Humes High School, however, Elvis gradually began to change. He grew his hair long and greased it back into the style known as a "Duck's Ass." As soon as he could grow them, he began sporting long sideburns. To make himself stand out even more, Elvis began wearing outlandish clothing—usually anything in pink or black, the louder the better. With some of the money from a part-time job at the Loew's State Theatre (he gave most of

his earnings to his mother), Elvis bought a collection of the flashiest clothing in Memphis. He bought most of his clothing at Lansky Brothers, a store he would frequent for the rest of his life. Lansky Brothers was on Beale Street, considered the home of the Memphis Blues, and also the edge of one of the toughest Black neighborhoods in town. Many local blues musicians used to frequent Lansky's, so undoubtedly Elvis experienced considerable contact with the Black music scene simply by hanging out on Beale Street.

While Elvis's flashy appearance tended to isolate him somewhat from his peers, it also lent him an air of notoriety. This was the 1950s, when crew cuts and conformity were in. Perhaps Elvis, already alienated because of his shyness and being a "cracker" in the big city, was searching for a sense of identity or a way of rebelling.

Despite Elvis's rebellious appearance, he did make at least a marginal attempt to fit in. In 1951, while a junior at Humes, he tried out for the football team, much to the chagrin of his overprotective mother. His cousin Earl Greenwood wrote that Elvis really wanted to make the team; however, he wasn't a very good player and he eventually quit when the coach ordered him to get a haircut. A few weeks after Elvis left the team, a gang of students gathered outside after school to hassle him. Red West, a star of the football team, noticed that Elvis was in trouble and came to his rescue. This would not be the last time that Red would help Elvis out of a scrape. Red would later become Elvis's bodyguard and good friend, and a member of the infamous "Memphis Mafia," until their ultimate falling out during the mid-1970s.

Outside of playing his guitar at a few parties and for his mother, Elvis did little to establish himself as a singer during his high school years. At the beginning of 1953, during his senior year, Elvis performed in the Humes High School Minstrel Show, but only after much prompting by his homeroom and history teachers. He sang the John Lair song, "Keep Them Cold Icy Fingers Off of Me," and reportedly got a standing ovation that lasted until he came out to do an encore—"Till I Waltz Again With You." It is interesting to note that Elvis's name was misspelled as Prestly in the Minstrel Show program.

In June 1953, Elvis Presley graduated from Humes High School, and one month later, took the best job he could find— driving a truck for the Crown Electric Company, located at 353 Poplar Avenue in downtown Memphis. His job mainly consisted of

Major: Science, Special Studies, Drafting, English.
Activities: Thespian, National Forensic, Debate Team, Spanish Club, Hi-Y, Biology Club, History Club, Speech Club, Student Council Representative, Non-Com Officer in R. O. T. C., Vice-President Speech Club, Vice-President History Club.
Awards: Winner District Debate Tournament, Winner "I Speak For Democracy" Contest.

ROBINSON, KATIE MAE
Major: Commercial, Home Ec., English.
Activities: F. H. A., History Club, English Club, Vice-President History Club.

RULEMAN, SHIRLEY

Major: Home Ec., Commercial, English.
Activities: National Honor Society, F. H. A., Y-Teens, Latin Club, Jr. Cheerleader, Sabre Club, History Club, English Club, Honorary Captain in R. O. T. C., President Home Ec. Class.

PRESLEY, ELVIS ARON

Major: Shop, History, English.
Activities: R. O. T. C., Biology Club, English Club, History Club, Speech Club.

PERRY, ROBERT EARL

Major: History, Science, English.
Activities: Biology Club, T&I Club, Key Club, Baseball 4 years, Vice-President Key Club, Boys' Vice-President Senior Class, President T&I Club.
Awards: All-Star American Legion Baseball Team 1952, National Honor Society.

SANDERS, MARY LOUISE

delivering electrical supplies to construction sites with the company's Ford F-100 pickup truck. Elvis used part of his weekly $41 salary to pay for an electrician's class at night, although he gave most of the money to his mother. Ironically, a few years before Elvis drove the Crown Electric truck, rockabilly star Johnny Burnette had held the same job.

While Elvis privately dreamed about becoming a singer, his public ambitions were far more practical. He enjoyed the freedom of driving a truck. In fact, he quit an earlier job as a factory worker at the Precision Tool Company in favor of the lower-paying job with Crown Electric. Possessed of a typical Southern boy's obsession with automobiles, Elvis's biggest hope was to some day own his own gas station, so he could "mess around with all sorts of cars." As he once told his cousin Earl, "I don't need that much money—jes' enough for me and Mama to get by on."

While driving the truck to work every day, Elvis used to pass the Memphis Recording Service, located at 706 Union Avenue. The Memphis Recording Service was started in 1950 by a former

Elvis's senior picture from the 1953 *Herald*, the Humes High School yearbook.

Personality Photos, Inc.

Elvis's extravagant dress and charismatic demeanor made quite an impression on Marion Keisker at the Memphis Recording Studio. Here, Elvis relaxes with his parents, Vernon and Gladys.

DJ named Sam Cornelius Phillips. Phillips started the studio to primarily record local Black rhythm and blues artists.

"It seemed to me," Phillips recalled, "that the Negroes were the only ones who had any freshness left in their music, and there was no place in the South where they could go to record..."

Phillips was under contract to provide recorded material for two record labels: Chess in Chicago and Modern in Los Angeles. Some of the more famous rhythm and blues artists to have recorded in Phillips's studio include Ike Turner, Jackie Brenston, Rosco Gordon, B.B. King, and Howlin' Wolf. Phillips had also recently started up his own record company, Sun Records, in order to expand into White country and western music.

One of the more lucrative sidelines of the Memphis Recording Service was expressed in their company motto "We Record Anything—Anywhere—Anytime." "Anything" included weddings, birthday parties, public speeches, and anyone willing to come in and pay four dollars to sing a song. The recordings were made directly onto acetate discs, which the singer could take home as soon as the taping was finished.

His curiosity aroused, Elvis stopped into the Memphis Recording Service with his guitar in hand in late August 1953. The studio waiting room was crowded with people waiting to record their songs. Sam Phillips's assistant, Marion Keisker, was running the booth that day. Elvis told her that he wanted to record two songs as a birthday present for his mother. This is highly unlikely, since Gladys's birthday had occurred four months earlier. Elvis would later admit, "I went to Sun, paid my four bucks to the lady because I had a notion to find out what I really sounded like. I had been singing all my life and was kind of curious."

Marion Keisker struck up what is now a very famous conversation with the young Elvis Presley while he anxiously waited his turn to sing.

"What kind of singer are you?"

"I sing all kinds."

"Who do you sound like?"

"I don't sound like nobody."

"Do you sing hillbilly?"

"Yeah, I sing hillbilly."

"Who do you sound like in hillbilly?"

"I don't sound like nobody."

As Marion Keisker and the world would soon find out, Elvis Presley really didn't "sound like nobody."

When his turn came, Elvis Presley sang the early Ink Spots hit, "My Happiness." Midway through the song, Marion Keisker noticed something unique about Presley's voice and started a tape machine to make a back-up copy to play for Sam Phillips.

As Marion Keisker told Elvis biographer Jerry Hopkins, "The reason I taped Elvis was this. Over and over I remember Sam saying, 'If I could find a white man who had the Negro sound and the Negro feel, I could make a billion dollars.' This is what I heard in Elvis . . . what they now call soul."

For the flip side of the record, Elvis sang another Ink Spots ballad, "That's When the Heartaches Begin," which Keisker captured in its entirety on the back-up tape. The original tape of these two songs has been lost; however, in 1988, the original acetate disc turned up in the home of Ed Leek in Memphis. Leek claims that it was he who originally encouraged Elvis to go to the Memphis Recording Service and that Presley brought the disc over to his East Jackson Avenue house immediately after recording it to play it for Leek and his grandmother. Leek says that Elvis left the disc there and never asked for it back. Apparently, he was not too thrilled with the result. Elvis described the recording as sounding like "somebody banging on a bucket."

Keisker took Elvis's address and the phone number of the rabbi who lived downstairs (the Presleys did not have a phone), and promised to call the young man if anything came up. When she played the tapes for Sam Phillips, he was not overly impressed. He liked Presley's voice, but didn't notice anything special about it.

Four months later, on January 4, 1954, Elvis went back to the studio to record two more songs. This time Phillips himself was at the controls. Elvis sang "Casual Love Affair" and a 1951 hit by Clint Horner called "I'll Never Stand in Your Way."

Phillips remained unimpressed. Over the next several months he did not bother to call Elvis in to make a demo, despite the urging of Marion Keisker. In June of that year, Phillips received a demo tape from Peer Music in Nashville of a Black singer performing a song called "Without You." He was so taken by the demo that he was prepared to release the tape as is. The only problem was that nobody knew who the singer was—he was just some kid who had been hanging around the studio that day. Marion Keisker described the recording as "a single voice with a single guitar, a simple, lovely ballad."

After giving up the thought of ever locating the vocalist, Phillips decided to find somebody else to sing the song. Keisker was finally able to convince him to give young Presley a call. According to Phillips, Elvis was over at the studio almost before he had hung up the phone.

Despite many attempts, Elvis was unable to master the intricacies of the slow ballad. He became extremely frustrated and even cursed the kid who had originally sung the song so well. After several hours, Phillips realized they were getting nowhere, so he asked Elvis what he could sing. Presley immediately started running through virtually every song he knew. This time Phillips saw a little more promise in Elvis. While he realized the kid was rough around the edges, he did see potential in Elvis's voice and demeanor.

Phillips put Elvis in touch with Scotty Moore, a young guitarist who played in a country and western band called Doug Poindexter and the Starlight Wranglers, with bassist Bill Black. Phillips realized that Moore would be a natural complement to young Presley. He had an interesting electric-guitar sound and a flowery, exuberant playing style. In addition, Moore and Phillips had previously had many lengthy conversations about developing a new popular music style—one that would unite the country blues, gospel, and pop elements of both White and Black music. Phillips thought (rightly so) that Elvis's unique singing style would blend in perfectly with this new music.

After recording his first records, Elvis, Scotty Moore, and Bill Black played extensive live dates throughout the south. The ferocity of the band's brand of rock and roll was surpassed only by the energy Elvis exuded on stage.

Archive Photos

On Sunday, June 27, 1954, Elvis went over to Scotty Moore's house, where he met Bill Black and the three of them went through a few songs. Moore later recalled that he thought his wife was going to "go out the back door" when she first saw Elvis, attired in his pink shirt and black and pink pinstripe pants, white shoes, and ducktail haircut. Presley, Moore, and Black talked for a little while and then ran through a dozen or so songs together. It has been reported that among the songs they played that day were "I Really Don't Want to Know," "I Apologize," "I Don't Hurt Anymore," and an Arthur "Big Boy" Crudup number called "That's All Right (Mama)."

Although by no means sold on Elvis as a singer, Moore and Black liked what they heard enough to stick with him for a while to see if anything happened. On July 5, Elvis went back into Sam Phillips's studio; this time, however, to record a commercial record with Scotty Moore and Bill Black. The first song the new band tried was "Harbor Lights," a 1937 ballad written by Jimmy Kennedy and Hugh Williams, made famous by Sammy Kaye in 1950. Phillips wasn't happy with the way the song was coming off. Presley's voice and the musicianship were there, but the sound offered nothing original, nothing new. (Phillips never did release this take of "Harbor Lights"; in fact, it was not released until 1976 when RCA came out with *Elvis—A Legendary Performer, Volume 2*. In 1980, the *National Enquirer* sent a copy of Elvis singing "Harbor Lights" to several record companies in Nashville, telling them it was a demo tape by an unknown artist. It was rejected by all of them).

After many more songs and several hours had passed, Phillips began to wonder if he had made a mistake with Elvis. Then, during a break from recording, Elvis began playing an upbeat version of the "Big Boy" Crudup blues standard "That's All Right (Mama)." More joking around than anything else, Elvis began dancing and bopping around the studio as he slapped his acoustic guitar and sang the song. Moore and Black quickly joined in on the fun, and pretty soon the three of them began rocking around the studio.

About midway through the song, Sam Phillips came rushing out of the control room.

"What in the devil are you doing?" Sam cried.

"We don't know," was the band's response.

"Well, find out real quick, and don't lose it. Run through it again and let's put it on tape."

Motion Picture & TV Archives

Sam Phillips knew that they were onto something with this song. It had the mixture of country and blues and Black and White that he had been looking for all along. He had finally found his "white man who had the Negro sound and the Negro feel." Over the next several months, Phillips, Presley, Moore, and Black spent many hours in the studio working on and perfecting their new sound. While Phillips is correctly given much credit for the development of Elvis's early sound, the roles played by Scotty Moore and Bill Black should not be underestimated. Without Moore unleashing those flowing guitar flourishes from his Gibson Electric hollow-body guitar, and without Black's bold and adventuresome bass licks on his stand-up, the "Elvis Presley sound" might never have come about.

Ultimately, however, it was Elvis himself who had the most to contribute to this new form of music. It was his voice and his energy that could pump new life into such tired old blues songs as "That's All Right (Mama)." Working essentially by instinct and motivated by a drive for success and respect, Elvis Aron Presley stumbled upon a new form of music that would soon set the country on its ear.

Elvis's dangerous good looks, deep voice, and sexually suggestive movements combined to provide the perfect antidote for teenagers fed up with the rigid mores of the 1950s.

"If I could find a white man who had the Negro sound and the Negro feel, I could make a million dollars."

—Sam Phillips

Personality Photos, Inc.

chapter two

THE SUN SESSIONS

In describing how he developed his gyrating stage demeanor, Elvis said, ". . . my manager told me that they [the audience] was hollering because I was wiggling. And so I went out for an encore, and I did a little more. And the more I did, the wilder they went."

Personality Photos, Inc.

With Sam Phillips at the controls, Elvis Presley, Scotty Moore, and Bill Black finished their first single on Monday, July 5, 1954, with "That's All Right (Mama)" on the A side and "Blue Moon of Kentucky" on the B side. Two days later, Phillips delivered an acetate disc of the record to Dewey Phillips, a DJ for WHBQ, who had a rhythm and blues program called "Red Hot and Blue." On Wednesday, July 7, 1954, Elvis Presley got his first radio play. Dewey Phillips was so enraptured by the fresh new sound of the Presley record that he played it over and over again. Pretty soon the radio-station switchboard began lighting up with calls requesting "That's All Right (Mama)." Practically everyone listening wanted to find out, "Who was this Elvis Presley kid?"

In the meantime, Elvis had been too nervous to listen to his own debut on the radio. After tuning in the correct radio station for his parents, he took off to Suzore's No. 2 Theater to see a Western double feature.

Once the requests and phone calls started coming into the radio station, Dewey Phillips knew that it was crucial that he interview Elvis Presley immediately. Phillips wanted to establish the fact that Elvis had gone to Humes High School so that everybody listening would know that he was White. Phillips got hold of Vernon, who went over to the theater to get Elvis.

According to Phillips, "Elvis came running in. 'Sit down, I'm gone interview you,' I said. He said, 'Mr. Phillips, I don't know nothing about being interviewed.' 'Just don't say nothing dirty,' I told him.

"He sat down, and I said I'd let him know when we were ready to start. I had a couple of records cued up, and while they played we talked. . . . Finally I said, 'All right, Elvis, thank you very much.' 'Aren't you gone interview me?' he asked. 'I already have,' I said. 'The mike's been open the whole time.' He broke out in a cold sweat."

Elvis surely had reason to be nervous. There was absolutely no way to predict how the White Southern population was going to react to this new sound. Guitarist Scotty Moore was sure they would be run out of town. Sam Phillips had hoped the record would cause controversy. Elvis, Scotty, Bill, and Sam had hit upon an entirely new sound, one that completely crossed racial barriers. In the White South of the 1950s, this was playing with dynamite. And while Presley's music was immediately accepted by a portion of the young population of Memphis, it was rejected as "nigger" music by the older, more conservative, White Southerners. In his book, *Elvis,* one of the most intelligent biographies written on Presley, *Rolling Stone* writer Dave Marsh describes the Elvis Presley controversy and success this way: "The crime of

Personality Photos, Inc.

To the parents of the 1950s, Elvis Presley was a no-talent juvenile delinquent who promoted an obscene new form of music. To the decade's teenagers, however, he was an instant idol who provided a release from the repression of the era. Elvis simply viewed himself as a singer who was enjoying some unexpected success.

© FPG International Archive (top 3 photos)

Michael Ochs Archive

One of Elvis's first Sun recordings was a Roy Brown R&B song called "Good Rockin' Tonight." This series of photos was taken for an early promotional release.

STEREO **ELVIS PRESLEY**
INTERVIEWS AND MEMORIES OF:
The Sun Years

Elvis's rock and roll was that he proved that black and white tendencies could coexist and that the product of their coexistence was not just palatable, but thrilling."

And thrilling it was. "That's All Right (Mama)"/"Blue Moon of Kentucky," was an immediate hit in the Memphis area. Sun had orders for five thousand copies of the record before the master disc was even cut and before Sam Phillips had officially signed Presley to a contract. Elvis signed a managerial contract with Scotty Moore as well as a recording contract with Sun Records on July 12. On July 19, "That's All Right (Mama)"/"Blue Moon of Kentucky" (Sun 209) was officially released.

The record quickly became a hit in Memphis, climbing to number three on the local charts and selling more than twenty thousand copies. Nationally, however, it got minimal attention. Few DJs were willing to play the record. It was too hillbilly for some DJs and too Black for most others. *Billboard* magazine, however, did give Presley a favorable review, describing him as a "potent new chanter who can sock over a tune for either country or r&b markets."

Spurred by their limited success, Scotty Moore set up a live show for the trio at the Overton Park Shell. It was an all country music show headlined by Slim Whitman and Billy Walker. The concert was promoted by local DJ and promoter Bob Neal, the man who would soon become Elvis Presley's first manager. Billed as the Hillbilly Cat and the Blue Moon Boys, the band performed "That's All Right (Mama)" and "Blue Moon of Kentucky."

On August 10, Elvis performed in both an afternoon and an evening show at the Overton Park Shell, with Slim Whitman again the headline act. In the afternoon show Elvis sang two ballads, "That's When Your Heartaches Begin" and "Old Shep." Later that evening, however, he cranked it up a bit and sang "That's All Right (Mama)" and "Good Rockin' Tonight." Presley so worked up the crowd with his brief set that Webb Pierce, who was scheduled to go on after Elvis, refused to perform.

In an interview later, Elvis recalled, "Everybody was screaming and everything, and I came offstage and my manager told me that they was hollering because I was wiggling. And so I went back out for an encore, and I did a little more. And the more I did, the wilder they went."

The next step for the band was to go back into the studio and cut another single. On September 10, they recorded the 1948 Wynonie Harris rhythm and blues hit, "Good Rockin' Tonight," the

Bettmann Archive

song that had aroused the Overton Park Shell audience. On the flip side was the country pop hit "I Don't Care If the Sun Don't Shine." This song was originally written in 1949 for the Walt Disney film *Cinderella*, but it was never used. Presley's version included an uncredited percussion performance by Buddy Cunningham, who pounded out a beat on an empty record box.

"Good Rockin' Tonight"/"I Don't Care If the Sun Don't Shine" (Sun 210) was released on September 25, 1954. While the single received a favorable review in *Billboard*, it didn't sell very well outside the Memphis area. Even in Memphis, it reached no higher than number 32 on the charts and only briefly appeared at the bottom end of the national country music charts.

Country singer Slim Whitman was the headlining act at Elvis Presley's first stage performance on July 30, 1954 at Memphis's Overton Park Shell. Elvis, Scotty, and Bill were billed as the Hillbilly Cat and the Blue Moon Boys.

Opposite page: As Elvis's popularity grew, Sam Phillips had the young singer record more often for his independent label, Sun Records. Elvis recorded a total of eighteen songs for Sun. Ten of these songs were released on five Sun singles; the remaining songs were not released until after Elvis signed with RCA.

Elvis Presley performing "That's All Right" at the Louisiana Hayride in October 1954. This was the first of many Presley appearances on the famous radio show, which was broadcast throughout the south from Shreveport, Louisiana on station KWKH.

Because of his earlier success with "That's All Right (Mama)," Elvis was booked on two of the most prominent country music radio shows in the South; The Grand Ole Opry, broadcast by WSM in Nashville, and the Louisiana Hayride, broadcast on KWKH from Shreveport, Louisiana.

On October 2, 1954, Elvis, Bill, Scotty, and Marion Keisker drove to Nashville for Elvis's appearance on the Opry. Elvis awaited the show with a great deal of anticipation and nervousness. Since 1925, the Opry had been country music's most famous radio show. All of the South's musical greats had appeared on the Grand Ole Opry at some point during their careers,

including Hank Williams, Eddie Arnold, Hank Snow, Patsy Cline, Minnie Pearl, and hundreds more. Elvis was convinced that this appearance was his big break into the country music scene. Instead, the show turned out to be nothing short of a disaster. Elvis, Scotty, and Bill performed "Blue Moon of Kentucky" and "That's All Right (Mama)." The band's performance was more than adequate. They rocked through the tunes without mishap and Elvis gyrated around the stage in the same manner that had earned him the crowd's approval at the Overton Park Shell. The Grand Ole Opry, however, was a very traditional, pure country show. Elvis's quick-paced mixture of country and rhythm and blues was too much for the conservative Opry crowd. In one of the most infamous misjudgments in entertainment history, Opry manager Jim Denny told Elvis he should go back to driving trucks.

Elvis was devastated by the rejection. He became convinced that the little success he had enjoyed up to this point had abruptly ended. During the drive back to Memphis, Elvis talked to Scotty, Bill, and Marion about giving up singing and going back to electrician's school. Luckily for Elvis (and for the rest of the world), the band talked him out of it.

Presley was due to perform next on the Louisiana Hayride. Based in Shreveport, Louisiana, the Hayride was broadcast on Saturday nights throughout the South on radio station KWKH. Although it was consistently gaining in popularity, the Hayride was still considered a lesser cousin to the Grand Ole Opry. Elvis, Scotty, and Bill made the first of many appearances on the show in late October 1954. Once again, the trio performed "That's All Right (Mama)" and "Blue Moon of Kentucky." This time, however, they were a big hit. Indeed, the Hayride audience and management alike were so enthralled by Presley that they asked him back the next week and signed him to a one-year contract to make regular appearances on the show. The band was paid union scale for each appearance: $18 for Elvis and $12 each for Scotty and Bill. In addition to singing, Elvis read a few of the commercials for farm products and food that played on the show.

Spurred by the success of the Hayride, Elvis quit his job at the Crown Electric Company and decided to devote his life full-time to music. The band embarked on a non-stop touring schedule. They performed at bars, honky tonks, country music nightclubs, and fairs (sometimes simply playing off the back of a flatbed truck) across the South. Travelling from Florida to New Mexico, the band played at practically any venue that would hire them. With each performance, the Elvis Presley following grew. With his greased hair, black-and-pink suits, curled lip, and gyrating hips, Elvis exuded a sexual aura that at once attracted and served as a release for the repressed youth of the 1950s. Presley did on stage what was considered improper for young people of the day to even think about, and as a result, women went crazy over him. Every place he performed he was greeted by hysterical, screaming throngs of women, who grabbed at him and tore at his clothing, often fainting from overexcitement. No other performer —except perhaps Frank Sinatra or Rudolph Valentino—had ever before elicited such a strong reaction from a female audience.

Wide World Photos

The male audience, however, was a different story. While many young men could relate to Presley's brazen sexuality (they saw in Presley a sexual ideal that society would not let them emulate), many others saw him as a threat to their manhood. A number of young Southern males became very jealous of and angry at Elvis because of the way their girlfriends reacted to him. Elvis was frequently threatened and even attacked by jealous boyfriends for the way he sang to their dates or for just being too sexy.

On December 10, 1954, Elvis, Scotty, and Bill went back into the studio to record their third single. The A side was "Milkcow Blues Boogie," a 1935 rhythm and blues song written by James "Kokomo" Arnold with the title "Milk Cow Blues." On the B side was "You're A Heartbreaker." This Jack Alvin Sallee tune was originally recorded in 1953 by country singer Jimmy Heap. "Milkcow Boogie Blues"/"You're A Heartbreaker" (Sun 215) followed a formula that had been successful on Elvis's first two singles—a rocked-up rhythm and blues song on the A side with a country-oriented B side. The band's sound and style was acquiring definition and shape. The songs were beginning to rock a bit harder and the Presley/Moore/Black/Phillips brand of rock and roll was coming to the forefront. As Dave Marsh points out: "Elvis, Scotty, Bill and Sam built their music in the recording studio, the first time anyone had ever created a major musical innovation except by working it out in front of a live audience or by laboriously composing it on paper first. Magnetic recording tape had only recently made it possible to do a take of a song, listen to the playback, analyze it, then try another rendition..."

While "Milkcow Blues Boogie"/"You're a Heartbreaker" marked a continuation in the development of the Elvis Presley sound, it didn't do particularly well in sales. It made little headway on the music charts and was never reviewed in *Billboard*.

While his record sales had begun to slide, Elvis's live performances remained as popular as ever. On January 1, 1955, at the insistence of both Sam Phillips and Scotty Moore, Elvis hired Memphis DJ and promoter Bob Neal as his first full-time manager. Born in the Belgian Congo in 1917, Neal had moved to the United States with his family in 1930. In 1940, he was hired as a disc jockey for WMPS radio in Memphis and soon had his own show: "The Bob Neal Farm Show." In addition, Neal owned the Bob Neal Record Shop on Main Street in Memphis. In 1952, he entered the promotions field when he established the Memphis Promotions Agency, located at 160 Union Avenue.

As Presley's manager, Neal was primarily concerned with booking shows for Presley. For this service he received 15 percent off the top of all money Elvis earned. After Neal's share and expenses were deducted, Elvis would split the remainder with Scotty and Bill—Elvis receiving 50 percent and Scotty and Bill getting 25 percent each. At the time, the band was making approximately $200 to $400 per appearance.

Neal booked Elvis on his first major tour in May 1955. It was a three-week stint featuring Mother Maybelle and the Carter Sisters, The Wilburn Brothers, Slim Whitman, Faron Young, and Hank Snow. The tour hit all of the major markets in the South—Nashville, Houston, Dallas, New Orleans, Richmond, St. Louis—as well as many smaller stops in between. At the same time, Sun Records released Presley's fourth single: "Baby Let's Play House"/"I'm Left, You're Right, She's Gone" (Sun 217). Record sales were extremely strong in the cities where the tour stopped. More importantly, these sales began to carry over into the national market as well. "Baby Let's Play House" turned out to be Elvis's breakthrough single. The song reached number 10 on *Billboard*'s Country chart—remaining on the chart for 15 weeks—and number 5 on the Country Disc Jockey chart.

Sun followed the success of "Baby Let's Play House" with the release of "Mystery Train"/"I Forgot to Remember to Forget" (Sun 223) in August 1955. "Mystery Train," written by Herman "Little Junior" Parker and Sam Phillips in 1953, was based on the 1930 Carter Family song "Worried Man Blues." Presley's recording featured the usual band of Elvis, Scotty Moore, and Bill Black,

Elvis's third record was "Milkcow Blues Boogie"/"You're a Heartbreaker" (Sun 210). Sam Phillips followed the same formula with all of Elvis's Sun records—a rocked-up rhythm and blues song on the A side with a country-oriented song on the B side.

Michael Ochs Archive

with the addition of Johnny Bernero on drums.(D.J. Fontana would begin playing drums for Elvis later on in 1955 and continue until 1969 when he quit to become a session drummer in Nashville. Fontana didn't play, however, on any of Presley's Sun recordings.) "Mystery Train" proved a suitable follow-up to "Baby Let's Play House," reaching number 11 on *Billboard*'s Country Music chart.

By this time, the world was beginning to take note of Elvis Presley. *Billboard* magazine named him the eighth most-promising Country and Western vocalist and stated that he was "the hottest piece of merchandise on the Louisiana Hayride." DJs across the country were suddenly playing Presley records with a determined regularity. A new youth music movement was sweeping the country. In Cleveland, DJ Alan Freed dubbed the new music Rock and Roll, and Elvis was quickly establishing himself as the movement's forerunner.

All of this attention got Elvis an audition for "Arthur Godfrey's Talent Scouts," the most popular talent-search program of the 1950s. Elvis Presley and the Blue Moon Boys, as they were billed at the time, were flatly rejected after they played "Baby Let's Play House" for Godfrey and the judges. Pat Boone auditioned for the same show and was accepted, ultimately winning first prize. Two years later, Buddy Holly and the Crickets auditioned for the show and were also turned down. Clearly, Godfrey had no ear for rock and roll. The show was canceled in 1958.

Another person who took notice of Elvis Presley's early successes was Colonel Tom Parker, a former carny barker turned country music manager. Colonel Parker, whose real name was Andreas Cornelius van Kuijk, was born in Breda, Holland, on June 26, 1909. He lived there until 1929, when he illegally emigrated to the United States, changed his name to Tom Parker and claimed Huntington, West Virginia, as his place of birth. (One of the reasons Elvis Presley never toured Europe or Japan was because Parker, an illegal immigrant, could not obtain a passport for fear of getting caught and being deported). Parker served three years (1929 to 1932) in the Army with the 64th Coast Artillery. He married Marie Mott Ross in 1932, and then began his career working in travelling fairs and carnivals as a barker and sometime con man. Two of his more infamous acts were the "Great Parker Pony Circus" and "Colonel Parker and his Dancing Chickens." In the latter act, Parker placed live chickens on a hot plate covered with sawdust. The reason the chickens danced was not because of the music, but to keep from burning their feet.

Parker had originally gotten into the music business in the 1940s, when he promoted a few shows for singer Gene Austin. Parker's favorite promotion gimmick was to blanket a town with flyers and posters for several weeks before the singer's scheduled appearance, thus making even a minor star appear important. Parker went on to manage country music legend Eddie Arnold from 1942 to 1951, as well as one of Elvis Presley's idols, Hank Snow, from 1954 to 1956.

The Colonel immediately saw a great deal of potential in Elvis; however, he knew that Presley needed more seasoning before hitting the big time. Like any good confidence man, Parker bided his time. He knew he wanted Presley for a client, but he didn't want to rush into anything, either. Besides, Parker knew that Presley was under contract with Bob Neal, at least for the time being. Parker saw how influenced the young Elvis was by his parents, especially his mother, so the Colonel began making inroads with Vernon first and then, with much more care, Gladys. In the summer of 1955, Parker approached Bob Neal about promoting a few shows for Elvis through his promotion company, All Star Attractions. The overworked Neal gladly accepted the Colonel's generous offer.

Parker gradually worked his way into Elvis's life and career. He befriended Vernon, appealing to his greed and tempting him with promises of riches and stardom for his son. Gladys was slightly

Former carny barker and country music manager Colonel Tom Parker signed Elvis to a management contract on August 15, 1955. Parker would remain Elvis's sole manager throughout his career.

Beltmann Archive

While promoting Elvis, Parker was perhaps the most visible manager in the history of the entertainment world. Here, Parker makes the most of a photo opportunity as Elvis hands him his mustering out pay after being discharged from the U.S. Army on March 3, 1960.

less accepting of Parker. She didn't think he was a man who could be trusted, yet even she had to admit he had a superior business acumen. Parker began booking more and more of Elvis's shows, and by the end of 1955, he was set to take over as Presley's manager.

On August 15, 1955, Elvis signed a contract hiring Colonel Tom Parker as his sole manager. For his services, the Colonel would receive 25 percent of all the money Presley made. When Elvis signed the contract, he was still officially under contract with Bob Neal until March 15, 1956. In essence, when Elvis signed the contract with Parker he agreed to pay Parker 25 percent and Neal 15 percent in order to do the same job. Through the last several months of 1955, however, Neal was Presley's manager in name only. While Elvis felt a great deal of loyalty toward Neal, he was also smart enough to realize that Neal simply did not have the connections that Colonel Tom Parker had, and that if his career was going to continue to progress, the best choice was to sign with Parker.

After losing Elvis Presley, Bob Neal went on to form a management company called Stars, Inc., with Sam Phillips. In 1958, Neal became Johnny Cash's first manager. He also managed such rock and roll and country music greats as Carl Perkins, Jerry Lee Lewis, Roy Orbison, Conway Twitty, Sonny James, Warren Smith, and a slew of other Sun recording artists.

The first thing Parker did as Presley's manager was to get Elvis out of his Louisiana Hayride contract. While the Hayride had given Elvis plenty of good exposure throughout the South over the past two years, Parker knew that if Elvis was to hit it big, he would need the type of national exposure that the Hayride could not offer. Parker also realized that Elvis would have to leave Sun Records and sign with a major national label.

Sam Phillips was not blind to the writing on the wall. With Colonel Parker in the picture, Phillips knew that Elvis's days at Sun were numbered. Nor was Phillips completely averse to losing Elvis. Presley was on the verge of becoming a mammoth singing star. Parker, after getting Presley out of his Louisiana Hayride contract, had begun negotiating a major tour for Presley, as well as possible national television appearances. Sam Phillips knew that if Elvis were to have a really big national hit, it could virtually destroy a small record company like Sun Records. Phillips simply did not have the tremendous capital necessary to press and distribute a million-selling record. Besides, if Parker could arrange a lucrative deal with a major label, Sun Records would receive enough capital for Phillips to push his latest young prodigy, rockabilly singer Carl Perkins. Phillips felt that Perkins had at least as much, if not more, potential than Elvis Presley.

So with Phillips's consent, Colonel Parker went to New York to begin negotiating a major record deal for Elvis Presley. The only stipulation that Phillips gave Parker was that he not settle for less than $20,000. Three labels were seriously interested in the young sensation from Memphis—Columbia, RCA, and the fledgling Atlantic Records.

During the 1950s, RCA Victor and Columbia were the two giants of the record industry. In country music, Nashville was the capital, and RCA Victor controlled most of Nashville. Columbia desperately wanted to sign Elvis to gain a foothold in Nashville. The Columbia executives believed that Presley was the future of country music.

Atlantic, on the other hand, was a young, upstart record label started by Ahmet Ertegun—the son of a Turkish ambassador to the United States—and former *Billboard* reporter Herb Abramson. Focusing mostly on rhythm and blues artists, Atlantic had pulled a coup three years earlier by buying Ray Charles's contract from Swingtime Records for $2,500. Like Columbia, Atlantic saw Elvis as a way of establishing itself in the lucrative Nashville/country music market.

Of the three companies, RCA Victor was probably the least interested in buying Presley's contract. The executive who was pushing for Elvis was A&R man Steve Sholes. Sholes was responsible for signing such RCA/Nashville stars as Hank Snow, Eddie Arnold (two of Parker's clients), and Pee Wee King. He had seen Elvis on the Grand Ole Opry and knew he was something special.

Columbia was the first company to bid. A&R man Mitch Miller offered $15,000 for Elvis's contract. Had it been up to him, Sam Phillips might have taken the money, even though he had earlier stipulated that he wanted at least $20,000; Colonel Parker, however, was a shrewd negotiator and knew that more money was available elsewhere. Parker also knew that Mitch Miller was very outspoken against rock and roll music and that Elvis would not necessarily get the support he deserved at Columbia. Parker asked for $20,000, and Miller immediately refused, stating that no performer was worth that much money.

Next, Atlantic came up with a $25,000 bid. The money was right, but Parker was a little apprehensive about signing Presley to a relatively small independent label—even though its star was on the rise. Parker felt that if Atlantic spent $25,000 for Elvis then the company resources would be strained and it wouldn't have enough money to properly promote his records.

Over at RCA Victor, Sholes finally pressed the apprehensive company to take a gamble on Presley. Sholes believed in Presley enough to essentially stake his entire future as a record executive on Elvis's success. Had Presley failed, Sholes certainly would have been driven out of the music business. RCA bid $25,000 to buy out the contract from Sun Records and obtain the rights to all of Presley's Sun recordings (Phillips was allowed to sell out the remaining copies of the Presley records Sun had already pressed), plus another $5,000 advance to Elvis himself (Elvis used a portion of the money to buy his mother—who did not drive—a pink Cadillac).

At the same time, Colonel Parker negotiated the $15,000 buyout of Sam Phillips's Hi-Lo Music, which held the publishing rights to Elvis's music, by the New York-based Hill and Range Music Company. As part of the deal, Hill and Range set up two subsidiary companies, Gladys Music and Elvis Presley Music, in order to filter partial royalties from the actual songwriters to Elvis Presley and Colonel Parker. This music-publishing agreement is a perfect example of Colonel Parker's philosophy of going for the quick buck rather than cultivating an artistic career. With this arrange-ment, any songwriter who wrote a song for Elvis Presley (who didn't write songs on his own) would have to agree to give up a portion of his or her royalties. Because of this condition, many of the era's greatest songwriters stayed away from Elvis in order to hold on to their royalties. Some of the writers who did work for Hill and Range wrote many of the worst songs Elvis ever recorded, including most of the songs in his movies.

Elvis, Colonel Parker, and Sam Phillips finalized the agreement with RCA Victor and Hill and Range on November 20, 1955. The $40,000 total was the most ever paid for the recording and publishing rights to a singer. The expense also guaranteed that RCA Victor would do everything in its power to promote Elvis Presley and protect its investment. As RCA would discover, Presley was worth every penny of the investment. By the time of his death in August 1977, Elvis Presley would sell more than 500,000,000 records—far more than any other recording artist.

Through this deal alone, Colonel Parker catapulted Elvis Presley to the forefront of the modern music scene. Yet, Parker was far from finished. At the time of the RCA signing, the Colonel was already negotiating to bring Elvis Presley into the living room of nearly every household in North America, via national television.

As Parker once told Elvis: "You stay talented and sexy, and I'll make us both rich as rajahs."

The Colonel talks to former Olympic Champion Duke Kahanamoku while arranging for Presley's U.S.S. *Arizona* Memorial Fund Benefit Concert on March 25, 1961. The benefit would be Elvis's last live performance until 1969.

"When I met him, he only had a million dollars worth of talent. Now he's got a million dollars!"

—Colonel Tom Parker

chapter three

ELVIS
'56

Personality Photos, Inc.

After signing the largest recording contract in history, Elvis Presley went to Nashville where he recorded "Heartbreak Hotel," his first record for a major label.

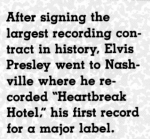

As 1956 began, Elvis Presley was on the verge of stardom—not just as a country and western singer, not as a white rhythm and blues enthusiast, and not as a Dean Martin–type crooning balladeer (his original ambition) but as a rock and roll teen idol such as the country had never seen before.

With the ink still drying on his new record contract, the twenty-one-year-old Elvis Presley set off for the RCA studios in Nashville to begin recording his first record for a major label. The first RCA sessions that took place on January 10 and 11 were produced by RCA Artists and Repertoire man Steve Sholes and the Nashville guitar legend Chet Atkins.

Atkins had come to Nashville ten years earlier from Luttrell, Tennessee. Steve Sholes had heard Atkins's recording of "Canned Heat" and was impressed by the young guitarist's virtuosity. Atkins quickly became a musical institution in Nashville through his own instrumental recordings, by backing other artists as a session musician, and later, as a producer. By 1960, Atkins had become RCA's A&R manager; by 1968 he was vice president.

Atkins said of Presley: "When he came along, he was so different in everything that he did. . . . He was the first to start the thing about rhythm. He dressed differently and moved differently

from anybody we had ever seen. He was electrifying. . . . I don't think there will ever be another like him."

Also backing up Elvis in that original RCA session were his road band—Scotty Moore, Bill Black, and newly added drummer D. J. Fontana—slip-note piano player Floyd Cramer, vocalist Gordon Stoker, leader of the gospel vocal quartet The Jordanaires, and background vocalists Ben and Brock Speer, members of the Speer Family vocal group.

All the Jordanaires, which consisted of Stoker, Neal Matthews, Hoyt Hawkins, and Hugh Harrett, would begin recording with Elvis on July 2, 1956. The vocal quartet sometimes referred to as "the sound behind the king," would soon become a permanent part of Elvis's recording and performing crew. The quartet formed in 1948 and quickly became a staple of the Nashville music scene by performing on the Grand Ole Opry and by backing such country and popular music legends as Red Foley, Hank Snow, Kitty Wells, Jim Reeves, Tennessee Ernie Ford, and in later years, Marie Osmond, Merle Haggard, and Tom Jones.

The first song Elvis put down on tape at RCA was the 1955 Ray Charles rhythm and blues hit "I Got a Woman." This gritty tune was true to the sound Elvis had developed at Sun; however, it was not the breakthrough hit that RCA was looking for. That would come shortly, with an original tune entitled "Heartbreak Hotel."

"Heartbreak Hotel" was written for Elvis by the songwriting team of Tommy Durden and Mae Axton. The inspiration for the song came in 1955 when the two noticed a headline in the Miami Herald asking "Do You Know this Man?" The story was about an unidentified well-dressed man who had committed suicide. He had no wallet and no papers on him except for a note he was clutching that read: "I walk a lonely street." Durden and Axton wrote a blues song centered around this idea and recorded a demo tape. Elvis first heard the demo when he was attending a disc jockey conference held in Nashville in November, 1955. He was so taken by the song that he vowed to record it the next time he was in the studio.

In an attempt to imitate the distinctive sound Elvis had developed at Sun, Chet Atkins wanted a heavy echo effect on the vocals. To achieve it, he had Elvis sing part of the song in the old stairwell of the building that housed the RCA offices. The resulting sound was so unusual that RCA and Colonel Parker almost didn't allow it to be released, describing the recording as a "morbid mess."

Despite the worries about the sound, "Heartbreak Hotel" was released two weeks later, on January 27, 1956, with "I Was the One" on the flip side (RCA 47-6420). Within a month the single jumped into the top forty on the *Billboard* Popular Music chart. By April, "Heartbreak Hotel" had bumped "The Poor People of Paris" by Les Baxter out of the number one spot. The song also reached number one on the *Billboard* Country Music Chart and the Rhythm and Blues Chart, the first song ever to reach number one on all three major *Billboard* charts. "Heartbreak Hotel" was also Elvis's first record to sell more than a million copies. To date, the record has sold more than 18 million copies. This "morbid mess" quickly catapulted Presley into the national spotlight.

Along with "Heartbreak Hotel," "I Got a Woman," and "I Was the One," Elvis recorded "I'm Counting on You," written by Don Robertson, and the 1953 Drifters hit, "Money Honey" in that first two-day recording session. These songs were not released until September of 1956 and none of them made near the splash that "Heartbreak Hotel" did.

One major reason for Elvis Presley's meteoric rise to stardom during 1956 was television. America was still fascinated with the relatively new invention. During the 1950s, the variety show was the most popular program on television—on which young performers could test their talents for all the country to see.

Colonel Parker knew that the best way to gain nationwide attention and respect for Elvis Presley was to get him on television. While his recorded music was new, fresh, and exciting, it was through live performances that Elvis was truly able to demonstrate the full extent of the electricity he could generate. The band continued to tour incessantly throughout the South, yet their appearances were limited mostly to country music venues and outdoor fairs. National television exposure was clearly necessary; without it, Elvis Presley might never have achieved his pinnacle as the "King of rock and roll."

As Elvis was recording his first cuts for RCA, Colonel Parker was negotiating for his premiere appearance on the *Stage Show Starring Tommy and Jimmy Dorsey*. Elvis originally signed to appear on *Stage Show* for four consecutive Sundays at $1,250 per show. The number of shows was later increased to six because of Presley's increasing popularity.

Chet Atkins, shown here in a 1956 publicity photo, was a guitar virtuoso turned A&R man for RCA. He produced and played on most of Elvis's early RCA recordings.

Bettmann Archive

Personality Photos, Inc.

Elvis Presley made his national television debut on the *Stage Show Starring Tommy and Jimmy Dorsey*. Here, Elvis is flanked by the two big band legends (Tommy to the left and Jimmy to the right.)

Produced by Jackie Gleason and hosted by big-band leaders Tommy and Jimmy Dorsey, *Stage Show* originally started as a 1954 summer-replacement series for *The Jackie Gleason Show*, but was later continued as a lead-in show for *The Honeymooners*. By 1956, however, the show's ratings were suffering badly. In order to boost ratings, Gleason hired the new rock and roll singing sensation from Tennessee.

At 8:00 p.m. on January 28, 1956, Elvis Presley made his debut on national television. Appearing on the same bill that

night were the June Taylor Dancers—an institution on both *Stage Show* and the *Jackie Gleason Show*—Sarah Vaughan, and Gene Sheldon, as well as Tommy and Jimmy Dorsey and their orchestra. Elvis, Scotty, Bill, and D.J. provided quite a contrast to the slick, glitzy, champagne veneer of the rest of the show. After an introduction by Cleveland disc jockey Bill Randle, Elvis and the band rocked through versions of "Shake, Rattle, and Roll" and "I Got a Woman" with Elvis doing his customary gyrating and shaking across the stage. As was rapidly becoming the norm

36

Best Wishes
Elvis Presley

Personality Photos, Inc.

Elvis's TV appearances made him one of the most recognizable faces in the country. This autographed photo was taken in 1956.

Opposite page, top: Elvis's custom-made hand-tooled guitar, which he used for most of his television appearances and live performances was a far cry from the $7.75 model his mother had bought him for his eleventh birthday. Opposite page, bottom: One feature that remained the same from his teens to his death was his dyed-black, slicked-back hair.

By 1956, Elvis Presley had become so famous that he could very seldom venture out into public during the daylight hours without causing a mob scene. This publicity photo was taken to show that Elvis, despite his fame, was just a simple southern boy at heart.

Personality Photos, Inc.

during an Elvis Presley performance, the audience, which had a larger than usual teenage component that evening, went wild. Many of the teenage girls, overcome with excitement, were screaming and crying at virtually every motion made by the handsome young singer.

While Presley's appearance did manage to boost the viewer ratings of *Stage Show,* it was still out-performed by NBC's competing offering, *The Perry Como Show.* The show received a lot of viewer mail and press attention due to Presley, however, and with each of his five subsequent appearances, ratings continued to climb. Despite his elation with the higher ratings Presley attracted for the show, Gleason was quoted as saying of Presley: "He can't last. I tell you flatly. He can't last."

After Elvis's appearances on *Stage Show* ended, Colonel Parker immediately signed him up for two appearances on *The Milton Berle Show.* For eight years, "Uncle Miltie" had been the reigning king of television comedy; so much so that he was dubbed "Mr. Television." Berle's television career had begun in 1948, when he was the host and star of *The Texaco Star Theater.* The show's name was later changed to *The Buick-Berle Show* and finally, to *The Milton Berle Show.* After eight years, however, the ratings on Berle's show were beginning to slip. Just as Gleason had done with *Stage Show,* Berle signed Presley (to two shows, at $5,000 each) in an attempt to regain audience attention and to boost ratings.

The April 3, 1956 show was broadcast from the deck of the USS *Hancock,* which was docked in San Diego. Elvis performed three numbers, "Shake, Rattle, and Roll," "Heartbreak Hotel," and "Blue Suede Shoes." He also appeared in a brief comedy sketch in which Uncle Miltie played Elvis's twin brother, Melvin Presley. The audience for this show was estimated to have reached about forty million people.

With this and his subsequent appearance on "The Milton Berle Show" on June 5, 1956, Elvis was thrust firmly into the public eye. The Presley phenomenon could no longer be ignored. Television had taken him out of the jukeboxes and off the local stages and broadcast him, wiggling pelvis and all, right into the middle of the "American Living Room."

Elvis Presley was now a force to be reckoned with. "Heartbreak Hotel" and several of the re-released Sun recordings dominated the pop, country, and rhythm and blues charts. He was regularly appearing on television and his touring region grew wider. Teen-

Two typical Elvis fans were Cralee Davolt, age 15, and her younger sister Sharyn, 14, who papered the walls in their bedroom with 1,087 photos of the King. Elvis's live performances generally featured hordes of hysterical teenage girls. Here, an enthusiastic fan screams her approval at a Presley concert in Philadelphia.

Wide World Photos

Wide World Photos

agers across America were caught up in Presley mania. His sold-out live performances were packed with frenzied teenage girls who screamed, cried, and sometimes fainted at even the slightest sign of recognition from their revered star.

Elvis Presley represented the perfect fantasy figure for the repressed 1950s teenager. He was a poor Southern boy, who despite all odds, had made himself a star. He was six feet tall, dangerously handsome, and wore his hair long and slicked back into a DA. On stage, Elvis curled his lip, shook his arms, and thrust his hips. He radiated an open sexuality that was welcomed and admired by teenagers who had grown up in "the decade of conformity." He loved flashy clothing, Cadillacs, motorcycles, and rock and roll. Elvis Presley became an icon of teenage rebellion.

Teenage males admired him and teenage girls adored him. Crowds of fans held sentry outside his house, peering over hedges and through windows, hoping to catch a glimpse of him. After concert appearances, he was actually attacked by fans, who would tear at his clothing in an attempt to take a piece of him home with them.

Up until 1956, Presley's popularity had been primarily limited to the southern and southwestern United States. But with his appearances on *Stage Show* and *The Milton Berle Show* and his records topping the national charts, Elvis had landed very much in the national public eye. And while America's youth almost universally embraced Elvis Presley as the new musical messiah, many of the adults saw him as a dangerous threat to the country's

Elvis performs on Elvis Presley Day (September 26, 1956) at the Mississippi-Alabama Fair and Dairy Show, the site of his first public appearance twelve years earlier when he won second prize in the annual talent contest.

© Roger Marshutz/Motion Picture & TV Archives

In a way, it is ironic that many mainstream Americans saw Presley as a threat to their children. Behind the wild, primitive, thrill-seeking veneer, was a polite, honest, well-intentioned young man who drank nothing stronger than Pepsi, didn't smoke except for an occasional cigar, and referred to all of his elders as "sir" or "ma'am." Although he was 21 years old and nearly a millionaire, Elvis still lived with his parents in a modest, suburban, ranch-style house. Family was extremely important to Elvis. He had an unbreakable bond with his mother, and was to keep his family near him for the rest of his life. For entertainment, Elvis loved going to the movies, the amusement park, and the roller-skating rink. At this point in his life, however, Elvis could barely go out anymore. If he wanted to see a movie or go roller skating, he would rent the theater or the roller rink after hours and invite all of his friends along. This method of spending his leisure time started a pattern of staying up all night and sleeping all day that became a lifelong habit.

Bettmann Archive

Motion Picture & TV Archives

Above: Elvis hams it up with Irish "Sheena" McCalla on the *Milton Berle Show* on June 5, 1956. Right: The King signs autographs for a group of fans who would like to see him run for a higher office.

established values and morals. Religious leaders spoke openly about how Elvis Presley was a corrupting influence on teenagers. They perceived him as a delinquent who needed to be disciplined before he did irreversible damage to America's youth. In a 1956 feature on Presley, *Life* magazine described him as "a different kind of idol . . . deeply disturbing to civic leaders, clergymen, and some parents." The Reverend Charles Howard Graff of St. John's Episcopal Church in the Greenwich Village section of New York, described Presley as a "whirling dervish of sex." A few radio stations in the Midwest banned Presley's records and rock-and-roll music in general from the airwaves.

Personality Photos, Inc.

Regarding the moral controversy of which he was the center, Elvis seemed at times genuinely incredulous: "I don't see that any type of music would have any bad influences on people. I can't figure it out. I mean, how would rock and roll music make anybody rebel against their parents?"

Television and music critics at the time did not necessarily believe Elvis to be the devil incarnate, as did some of the clergy; instead, many thought of him as a talentless joke. After Presley's performance on *The Milton Berle Show, New York Times* critic Jack Gould wrote that Presley "has no discernable singing ability. . . . For the ear he is an unutterable bore. . . . His one specialty is an accented movement of the body that heretofore has been primarily identified with the repertoire of the blonde bombshells of the burlesque runway."

Critic John Crosby, writing in the New York *Herald Tribune,* described Elvis as "unspeakably untalented and vulgar," and Jack O'Brien of the New York *Journal-American* wrote that "Watching him is like watching a stripteaser and malted milk machine at the same time."

Elvis was instantly dubbed with a number of unflattering nicknames such as the "lurchin' urchin," "howlin' hillbilly," "southern shake," "baritone Marilyn Monroe," and, the one that stuck, "Elvis the Pelvis." Of this last nickname, Presley responded: "It's one of the most childish expressions I've ever heard comin' from an adult."

Yet despite all the attacks and condemnations, Elvis Presley's record sales continued to climb. By September of 1956, RCA announced that Presley records had sold more than 10 million

Elvis performs a song with guitarist Scotty Moore, bassist Bill Black, and drummer D. J. Fontana.

Wide World Photos

middle of a ratings war with *The Ed Sullivan Show* for the lucrative Sunday night 8:00 to 9:00 slot. This second version of *The Steve Allen Show* (Allen previously had a show that ran on NBC from 1950 to 1952) had premiered just one week before Presley's appearance, with Kim Novak, Sammy Davis Jr., and Vincent Price as guests. Allen put Elvis on his show as a way to boost his ratings while making fun of the "hillbilly rock and roller" at the same time.

Colonel Parker had originally tried to book Elvis on *The Ed Sullivan Show*; however, Sullivan responded to Parker's advances by flatly stating, "I wouldn't have him on my show at any price."

On July 1, 1956, Steve Allen opened his show wearing full evening dress. With his hair slicked back and his horn-rimmed glasses, Allen was dressed as the ultimate example of a fashionable New York "society" denizen. There was a muffled "bark" from offstage and then Allen introduced Presley:

"Well you know, a couple of weeks ago on *The Milton Berle Show*, our next guest, Elvis Presley, received a lot of attention— which some people seemed to interpret one way and some viewers interpreted another. Naturally, it's our intention to do nothing but a good show. We want to do a show the whole family can watch and enjoy and we always do. And tonight we are presenting Elvis Presley in his, what you might call his first comeback. And so it gives me great pleasure to introduce the new Elvis Presley."

Amid the by now customary cheers and screams, Elvis walked on stage wearing—much to the shock of the audience—formal evening dress, complete with white tails and blue suede shoes. Allen smugly presented Presley with a petition that had been organized by Tulsa, Oklahoma DJ Don Wallace requesting that he appear on television again "real soon." Elvis then broke into a rousing rendition of "I Want You, I Need You, I Love You," backed by the Jordanaires.

For the next act, the curtain opened to reveal the entire band. Allen, again wearing his smug country-club smirk, wheeled in a basset hound named Sherlock in a top hat. As humiliated as he may have felt, Elvis nevertheless, sang an inspired version of "Hound Dog" to the droopy-faced basset, grabbing the dog by the jowls and playing along with Allen's joke in good humor.

Later in the show, Allen brought Elvis back out to play a character named "Tumbleweed Presley" in a comedy skit entitled "Range Roundup," which featured Andy Griffith as "Rattlesnake

Elvis, Steve Allen, and Imogene Coca in a skit entitled "Range Roundup." On this show Allen had Elvis sing to a floppy-eared basset hound. Elvis greeted Allen's feeble attempts to humiliate him with good humor, although later he regretted appearing on the show in the way that he did.

units. Throughout it all, Elvis handled the press with a humble politeness that held true to his Southern upbringing, yet clashed with his rebellious image, stating simply: "I'm so grateful for all that's happened." And admitting: "I'm not kidding myself. My voice alone is just an ordinary voice. What people come to see is how I use it. If I stand still while I'm singin', I'm dead, man. I might as well go back to drivin' a truck."

One media personality who could not sit around without trying to debunk what he saw as the Elvis "myth" was television host Steve Allen. Allen was a self-styled cynic of the middlebrow who saw rock and roll as crude and uncultured. In 1956, he was in the

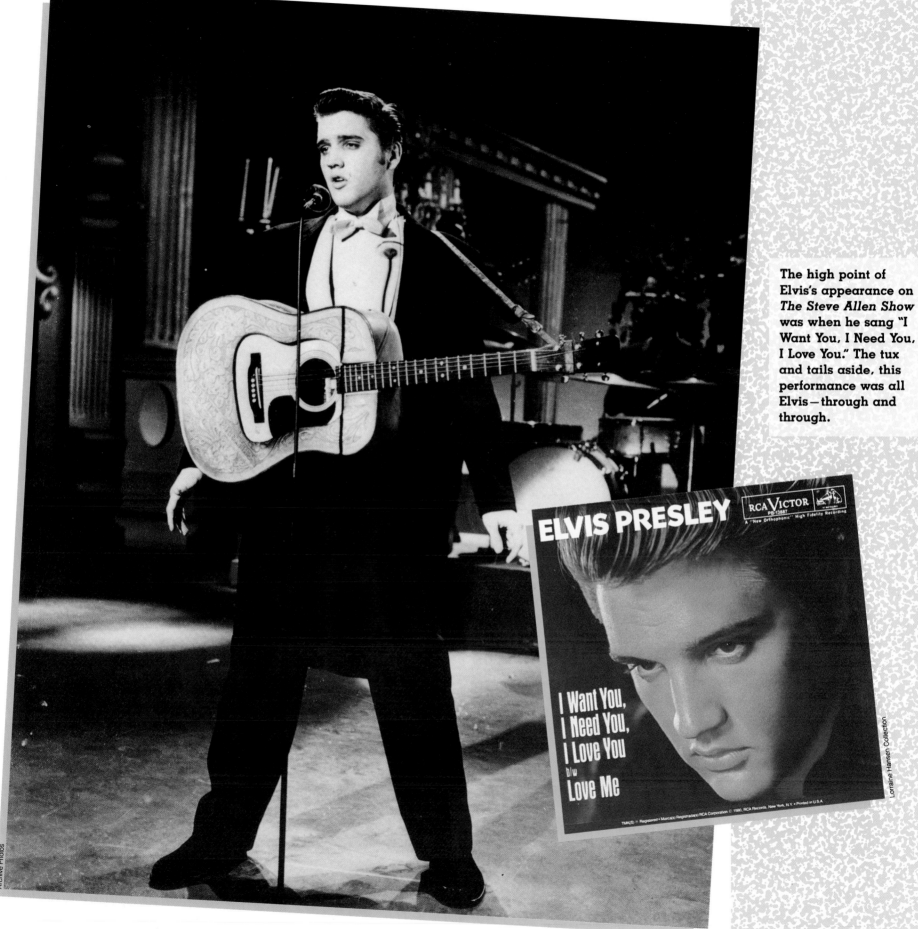

Archive Photos

The high point of
Elvis's appearance on
The Steve Allen Show
was when he sang "I
Want You, I Need You,
I Love You." The tux
and tails aside, this
performance was all
Elvis—through and
through.

ELVIS PRESLEY

RCA VICTOR
A "New Orthophonic" High Fidelity Recording

I Want You,
I Need You,
I Love You
b/w
Love Me

TMK(S) ® Registered • Marca(s) Registrada(s) RCA Corporation © 1980, RCA Records, New York, N.Y. • Printed in U.S.A.

Lorraine Hansen Collection

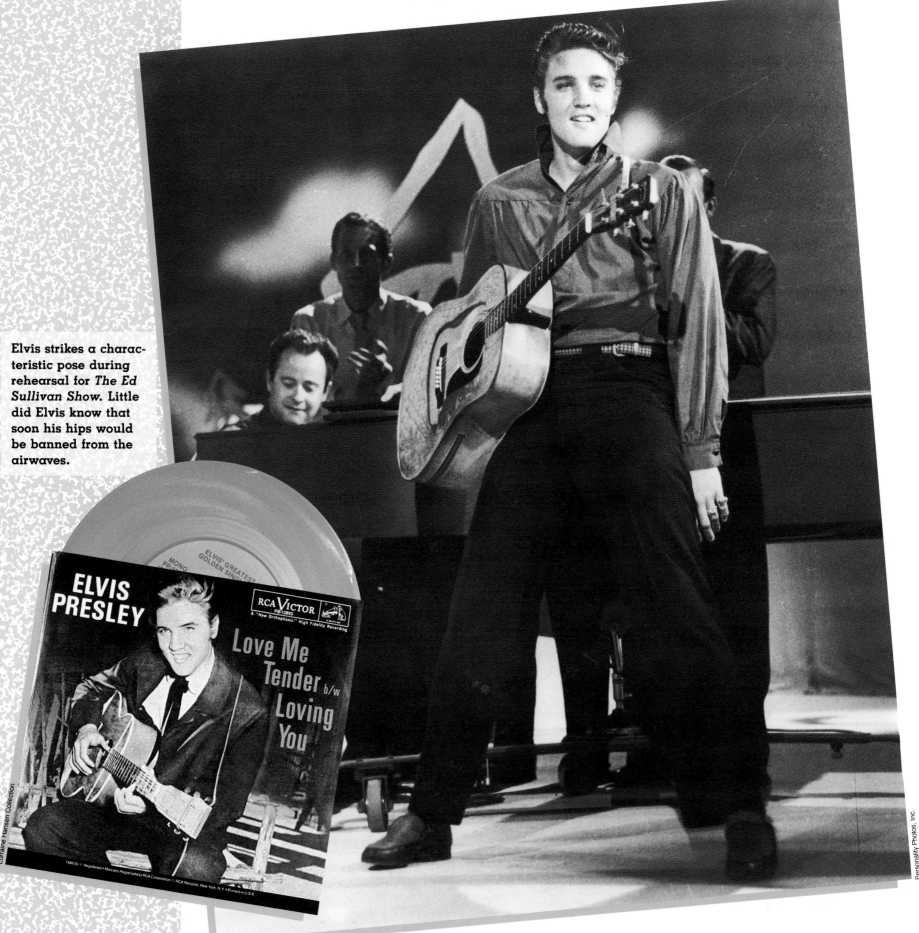

Elvis strikes a characteristic pose during rehearsal for *The Ed Sullivan Show*. Little did Elvis know that soon his hips would be banned from the airwaves.

ELVIS PRESLEY

Love Me Tender b/w Loving You

RCA VICTOR

Lorraine Hansen Collection

Personality Photos, Inc.

Griffith" and Imogene Coca as "Cactus Coca," the "little flower of the prairie." The skit consisted of a series of rambling, disjointed one-liners that attempted to make fun of poor Southerners and country and western music. The skit ended with Allen, Griffith, Coca, and Presley singing "Yippee Yi Yo Yi Yay."

Elvis later stated that he regretted appearing on the show the way he did, wishing instead that he had stayed true to his image. Allen got the ratings he was looking for—the show received a 20.2 rating as compared to Ed Sullivan's 14.8 that night—but his attempt to humiliate Elvis backfired. The following day, tried-and-true fans of Elvis protested in front of the studio with signs asking for the real Elvis Presley. Allen received angry letters for weeks following the show. Even John Lardner of *Newsweek* sided with Presley, writing "Allen's ethics were questionable from the start. He fouled Presley, a fair-minded judge would say, by dressing him like a corpse, in white tie and tails."

The one good result of the show was that it gained the attention of Ed Sullivan. Sullivan could no longer ignore the drawing power of Elvis Presley. Steve Allen had gotten 55 percent of the viewing audience that night as compared to a meager 15 percent for Sullivan. So, despite his earlier declaration against Presley, Sullivan signed him up for three appearances. True to form, Colonel Parker proved a tough negotiator. For his three performances Elvis received $50,000, far more than any other performer had ever received for appearing on a television variety show.

Television was the most important venue for a young recording star, and *The Ed Sullivan Show* was the pinnacle of television variety shows. Sullivan, a former newspaper columnist, ruled the lucrative Sunday-night market for twenty-three years.

Presley's first appearance on the Sullivan show was on September 9, 1956. The "Great Stone Face" himself was unable to appear on the show because he was recovering from a head-on automobile accident on August 6, near Seymour, Connecticut. Charles Laughton filled in for Sullivan as host. Elvis performed his segment of the show in a remote telecast from Hollywood—the rest of the show emanated from New York City. Elvis sang "Don't Be Cruel," "Love Me Tender," "Ready Teddy," and "Hound Dog." Other guests on the show included Dorothy Sarnoff, the Amen Brothers, the Vagabonds, and Indian vocalist Amru Sani.

The ratings for this first Presley appearance were astounding. The show had captured 82.9 percent of the entire viewing audience, or about four out of every five television sets. That trans-

Above: Elvis with an unidentified fan and Ed Sullivan during a rehearsal for the *Ed Sullivan Show* on January 6, 1956. Left: Elvis rehearses a song for the October 28 show.

Elvis gets ready to sing "Love Me Tender" on the *Ed Sullivan Show*.

of the finalists on that show was the rockabilly singer Johnny Burnette, a fellow Memphisite who had worked at the Crown Electric Company prior to Elvis's brief stint there.

When Elvis made his second appearance on Sullivan's show on October 28, Ed himself was there to introduce the new "King of rock and roll", although he never actually spoke to Elvis on camera. He did, however, briefly interview Robert Webb, the director of *Love Me Tender,* Elvis Presley's first movie. Elvis sang "Don't Be Cruel," "Love Me Tender," "Love Me," and "Hound Dog" and was presented with a Gold Record for "Love Me Tender."

Presley's third appearance on *The Ed Sullivan Show,* on January 6, 1957, was perhaps his most infamous. Sullivan had enjoyed extremely high ratings and had gained significant media attention by having the young rock and roller on the show. He was, however, getting a little nervous about the overt sexuality demonstrated in Presley's live performances. Elvis's swinging hips and throbbing pelvis were now headline material, much to the chagrin of PTA, church, and civic groups across the country. Sullivan became deeply concerned about a rumor that Elvis was stuffing something in his pants and was shaking it at the young girls. So, for the final performance, Sullivan ordered that Elvis be shot only from the waist up, successfully avoiding the whole "pelvis problem."

Sullivan's "censorship" made Presley more famous than ever. Now, Elvis was considered so hot that they could only show part of him on television. The waist-up filming also tempted and teased the audience more than if Sullivan had just ignored the controversy and taped him as before. Elvis moved the way he normally did, and the studio audience went just as crazy. But the audience at home could see only the upper half of Elvis, and by the screams of the audience, they knew that something pretty wild must have been going on down below.

On this appearance, Elvis performed "Hound Dog," "Love Me Tender," "Heartbreak Hotel," "Don't Be Cruel," "Too Much," "When My Blue Moon Turns to Gold Again," and "Peace in the Valley." At the end of the show, Ed Sullivan came out to say goodbye to Elvis and addressed the audience: "I wanted to say to Elvis Presley and the country that this is a real decent fine boy, and we've never had a pleasanter experience on our show with a big name than we've had with him." It remains unclear whether Sullivan made this statement of his own accord, or whether Colonel Parker "negotiated" it in recompense for the below-the-waist censorship of Elvis.

lated to a viewing audience of more than 50 million people. This was by far the highest-rated show in television history, a record that held steady until 1964, when The Beatles appeared on *The Ed Sullivan Show.*

Running opposite Presley that night was the National Amateur Talent Championships on *Ted Mack's Original Amateur Hour.* One

Personality Photos, Inc.

An autographed publicity still of Presley taken near the end of 1956.

When Elvis was young, he loved cars so much, he wanted to be a truck driver or to run a gas station. By 1956 he was rich enough to afford a whole fleet of Cadillacs. Opposite page: Elvis sits behind the wheel of a brand new, red Cadillac convertible.

Motion Picture & TV Archives

After the final Sullivan appearance, Colonel Parker raised the price of a Presley television appearance from $50,000 to $300,000. As a result, Elvis did not appear on television again until he returned from the Army in 1960.

Nevertheless, 1956 was truly the breakthrough year for Elvis Presley. He signed a major record deal with RCA, his records topped three major *Billboard* charts, and he was the most consistently played singer on the radio. His concerts regularly sold out, he was the rebel role model of teenage boys and the lustful fantasy figure of teenage girls, and to top everything off, he was the most-watched entertainer in the history of television. In little more than a year, Elvis Presley had gone from being a poor, struggling, part-time singer to being the millionaire king of the new musical movement known as rock and roll.

Presley did, however, have one failure during 1956. Colonel Parker booked Elvis to what was to be a two-week headline engagement beginning April 23 at the New Frontier Hotel in Las Vegas. During the 1950s, Vegas was perhaps the second biggest show biz town after New York. Parker felt that making a big splash in Vegas was essential to Presley's career.

The engagement was disastrous. Elvis attracted large crowds at first; however, the Vegas audiences were older and more conservative than those usually found at a Presley concert. The people came more out of curiosity than anything else, as if they were attending a circus sideshow. Missing were the screaming girls and the rabid fans; in their place was a crowd of sequined middle-class gamblers. After the first few shows, Elvis was dropped to second on the bill below comedian Shecky Greene. By the end of the first week, the Frontier mercifully agreed to tear up his contract. Upon leaving Vegas, Elvis vowed never to play in that town again, a promise he kept for more than ten years.

One good thing did happen while Elvis was in Las Vegas. He went to see a Black band named Freddie Bell and the Bellboys perform. He was so taken by their version of the 1953 Mama Thorton hit "Hound Dog"—to which they had added the lines, "You ain't never caught a rabbit. You ain't no friend of mine"— that he decided to add it to his own show. "Hound Dog" soon became such a popular live song for Elvis that he began using it to end his shows.

The song had been written by the songwriting team of Jerry Lieber and Mike Stoller in 1952 for rhythm and blues artist Willie Mae "Big Mama" Thorton. According to legend, the writers met Thorton at bandleader Johnny Otis's house and then quickly rushed back to Leiber's house, where they wrote the song in about eight minutes. Leiber and Stoller went on to write some of Presley's greatest post-Sun Records hits, including "(You're So Square) Baby, I Don't Care," "Jailhouse Rock," "Treat Me Nice," "King Creole," and "Loving You."

At the same time that Thorton's version of "Hound Dog"— originally about a gigolo—began making its way up the rhythm and blues charts, Sam Phillips wrote a nearly identical song called "Bear Cat" for Sun artist Rufus Thomas. The label of the

Personality Photos, Inc.

51

When asked why he moved the way he did on stage, Elvis candidly replied, "I'm not kidding myself. My voice alone is just an ordinary voice. What people come to see is how I use it. If I stand still while I'm singin', I'm dead, man. I might as well go back to drivin' a truck."

ELVIS PRESLEY
RCA VICTOR
A "New Orthophonic" High Fidelity Recording

Hound Dog
b/w
Don't Be Cruel

Lorraine Hansen Collection

Personality Photos, Inc.

record read "Bear Cat (the Answer to Hound Dog)" by Rufus "Hound Dog" Thomas. Phillips was sued for plagiarism and forced to pay a partial royalty to the publishers of "Hound Dog."

Elvis recorded "Hound Dog" on July 2, 1956 at RCA Studios, using the Jordanaires for vocal backing. The song was released on the B side of "Don't Be Cruel" (RCA 47-6604) and sold more than six million units in 1956 alone, staying on the *Billboard* Top 100 chart for twenty-eight weeks, peaking at number two. "Don't Be Cruel" was number one.

With all of his musical and television successes, there was only one area left in 1956 for Elvis to conquer—Hollywood. In March 1956, Colonel Parker placed ads in all of the Hollywood trade papers in the hopes of drawing the movie industry's attention to Elvis. A few months later, Elvis flew to Hollywood to do a screen test for Paramount Pictures producer Hal Wallis, whose many credits included *Casablanca.*

Wallis quickly signed Presley to a three-picture deal. Paramount agreed to pay Elvis $100,000 for the first picture,

$150,000 for the second, and $200,000 for the third with no percentages of the gross—an uncharacteristically soft deal by the Colonel's usually ruthless standards.

Elvis greeted the challenge of movie-making with both excitement and apprehension. Unsure as to whether he could truly act, Elvis was nonetheless thrilled with the prospect of becoming a movie star. Little did he know, however, that the signing of that three-picture deal would drastically change his public image, the direction of his career, and ultimately, his way of life.

Elvis had conquered the radio and television. The next step was for the King to head to Hollywood.

53

"This place is Elvis. You feel him here, and you always will. . . . Graceland remains a monument to him and the musical era he created."

—Jack Soden, Executive Director of Graceland

chapter four

GRACE-
LAND

Right: This plaque at Graceland commemorates the life of Elvis.

Opposite page: On March 26, 1957, Elvis bought his dream house for $100,000 cash. Graceland would remain his primary residence for the rest of his life, and the only place, he claimed, where he was truly happy.

By mid-1956, Elvis Presley was on the top of the entertainment world. He was the hottest draw on television, record stores had difficulty keeping the latest Presley releases in stock, his songs dominated the top-forty, country, and rhythm and blues radio stations, and he had just signed a three-picture deal with Hollywood producer Hal Wallis. In public, Elvis appeared to be the epitome of the flashy rock-and-roll playboy rebel. With his Lansky Brothers suits and chrome-trimmed Cadillacs, Elvis looked the part of the wild boy.

His private life, however, provided quite a contrast to his rebellious public image. When not on tour, Elvis lived with his parents in a small, rented, two-bedroom house (1414 Getwell Street) in a lower middle-class suburban neighborhood in Memphis. Although Elvis's clothing tended to be slightly more than gaudy, even when he was relaxing at home, the rest of his home life was almost boringly normal. His favorite pastimes were to sit on the stoop with his mother and drink Pepsi™ or to play with his dog in the backyard. (As of this writing, the current owner of the house on Getwell Street is having it dismantled and moved to make room for an auto-parts store. He hopes to eventually open the house to the public, and is currently selling souvenir bricks from the house for US$15 apiece.)

While the house on Getwell Street was the nicest home the Presleys had ever lived in, Elvis could now afford something much better. On May 11, 1956, Elvis bought a single-story, three-bedroom house at 1034 Audubon Drive in a fashionable, upper-class neighborhood just outside of Memphis. This house was by no means a flashy mansion. Yet, to a formerly poor rural family like the Presleys, 1034 Audubon Drive was a dream come true—a far cry from the low-income housing project of Lauderdale Courts where the Presleys had lived just three years earlier.

The new $40,000 ranch house was painted green with red brick trim and a grey roof. The flower-trimmed backyard held a large patio. Elvis later installed a pool (although he did not feel entirely competent in the water and rarely swam).

According to Earl Greenwood, in his book *The Boy Who Would Be King*, Gladys had her own plans for the backyard. Upon seeing the yard, Gladys exclaimed, "There's room back there for a decent-sized [chicken] coop, and we can get one of them new egg catchers. Durin' the day they could have the run of the yard. We'll need a rooster, too. Oh, when can we get them, Elvis?"

Much to the relief of the Presleys' conservative suburban neighbors—who were angry when Gladys hung her wash outside—Colonel Parker convinced Elvis and Gladys that it would not be a wise idea to put up a chicken coop in the backyard.

Elvis decorated the new house with bright, flashy furniture, gaudy, large print wallpaper, ceramic minstrels, and dozens of stuffed animals—an interior decorating style that reflected his taste in clothing.

It wasn't long after the Presleys moved into the new neighborhood that the fans found out where he was living. Soon there was a gathering of Elvis loyalists outside the house twenty-four hours a day. There was no fence around the small, half-acre lot, so fans would often come right up to the house and gaze into windows in hopes of catching a glimpse of the king. For the most part, Elvis didn't mind his fans hanging around. Although it deprived him of privacy, it was also a reassurance that his career was still taking off. Had the fans stopped coming, Elvis surely would have worried. Indeed, at first, Elvis frequently went out front to talk to his fans and to sign autographs.

By the beginning of 1957, however, the adulation was beginning to get out of hand. According to Earl Greenwood, Elvis was returning home after a rehearsal session one day when he saw the usual gathering of fans out in front of the house. He stepped out of his car and started to walk over to them to sign a few autographs. A screaming group of girls rushed toward Elvis, and soon the entire crowd bore down upon him, pinning him against the car. Elvis could not escape and the breath was being crushed out of him by the descending crowd. Luckily for Presley, his Uncle Vester saw what was happening and he and Vernon were able to pry Elvis loose. Once inside, Vernon told the visibly shaken Elvis that his fans were going to "love him to death."

The next day Elvis decided to hire his old friend and former Humes High School football player Red West as a bodyguard. He also encouraged Red to invite several of his friends along to accompany Elvis whenever he went out into public. This was the beginning of Elvis's famous entourage, later known as the "Memphis Mafia."

By March, 1957, Elvis realized that the house on Audubon Drive was neither private enough nor safe enough for him and his family to live in. In addition, the neighbors were constantly complaining about the masses of people gathered out in front of the house. So Elvis went shopping for a new house—one that included some land, had a gate to keep his fans at bay, and was big enough to comfortably house himself, his family, and whichever other members of the Memphis Mafia happened to be around at the time.

Elvis eventually found what he was looking for in the Whitehaven suburb of Memphis, a 13.5 acre (5.4 ha) estate and house known as Graceland.

Graceland was established as a farm during the American Civil War by T.E. Toof, a pressman for the *Memphis Daily Appeal*. The farm raised Hereford Cattle and originally encompassed more than 500 acres (200 ha) of the area today known as Whitehaven. Toof named the farmland Graceland after his daughter Grace

Motion Picture & TV Archives

Here, Elvis shows off his new home to actress Yvonne Lime on April 19, 1957. Elvis flew the young starlet in from Hollywood so that she could spend Easter weekend with him and his parents.

Toof, who inherited the land after her father died. The land was eventually handed down to Grace's niece Ruth, who had married a Memphis-area doctor named Thomas D. Moore.

Ruth and Dr. Moore built the current estate house in 1939. The rooms in the white Colonial-style house were built with superior acoustics because Ruth and her husband wanted to encourage their daughter Marie to become a musician. Indeed, Marie began playing the harp and the piano at age four. As an adult, she spent 15 years as a principal harpist for the Memphis Symphony Orchestra.

On March 26, 1957, Elvis Presley bought Graceland and the surrounding land for $100,000 in cash, outbidding the local YMCA by $65,000. The two-story house was built from tan Tennessee limestone and originally had twenty-three rooms, including five bedrooms. The room count of the house changed many times over the years that Elvis owned it due to numerous renovations.

When Elvis first showed the house to his mother, she could hardly believe that they were going to live there. To a poor country mother like Gladys, the white-columned house with a four-car garage and surrounding land spotted with full-grown, mature trees must have seemed like heaven on earth. Gladys was especially happy that Graceland was out in the country. In 1956, Whitehaven was not yet a populated suburb of Memphis. The area around Graceland was marked by rolling hills, farmland, and hedge rows. Gladys could finally have the chicken coop she had once wanted.

In six months, Elvis spent more than $400,000 remodeling the house. During the twenty years that Elvis lived in Graceland, the house and grounds were in a constant state of renovation. Elvis had the money and the means to turn Graceland into anything he wanted, no matter how outlandish.

Soon after moving in, Elvis ordered the exterior of the house painted blue and gold and arranged for it to be bathed in similarly colored spotlights to make it glow at night. The furniture he bought for the place was an eclectic mixture of 1950s modern and Louis XIV. He decorated the hallways with twinkling lights and painted clouds and added purple wallpaper to several of the rooms. Gold trim graced parts of every room in the house.

In 1957, Elvis installed the famous iron Music Gate in front of the house. The gate, designed for Elvis by John Dillars, Sr. of Memphis Doors, Inc., depicts the mirrored image of a man playing the guitar surrounded by musical notes, clefs, and graphs. Immediately after its installation the gate became a gathering place for many of the King's most loyal fans. They kept a constant twenty-four-hour vigil out front of Graceland. Elvis occasionally rode his golden palomino down to the gate to talk to his fans and sign autographs. Other times he would simply wave at the crowd as he drove through the gates on his way to a rehearsal or show.

Graceland remained Elvis's home for the rest of his life. It was there that he brought his bride, Priscilla, and it was the first home of his only child, Lisa Marie. Most of those who knew Elvis claim that Graceland was the only place he was ever truly happy. Indeed, the house proved to be an oasis for Elvis, a place where he could relax and escape the pressures of being the most famous entertainer in the world. Graceland was also the ultimate fantasy kingdom for Elvis. He ruled the house and surrounding land like a monarch. King of the castle, he created his own rules and his own lifestyle on the grounds, and anybody living at or visiting Graceland—of which there were many over the years— had to follow his rules.

The house was kept spotlessly clean and numerous air conditioners maintained a frigidly cold temperature. Due to his immense fame, Elvis was unable to go out in public during daylight hours. As a result, he developed an almost completely nocturnal existence. He would sleep until 4:00 or 5:00 in the afternoon, and then stay up all night, very seldom going out into the daylight, especially in his later years. Most of the windows in the house did not open and were kept shuttered to prevent sunlight from coming in. Elvis demanded a completely controlled environment. Even when he was on tour in his later years, he would have the windows in his hotel rooms lined with aluminum foil to prevent sunlight from coming in.

During the 1970s, Elvis very seldom ventured far from the gates of Graceland unless he was on tour. RCA had a difficult time even getting him to show up at recording sessions, so instead they brought a portable recording studio to him on two separate occasions in 1976. Some of the songs he recorded at these Graceland sessions include "Way Down," "Moody Blue," "Solitaire," and "Pledging My Love."

Elvis proudly poses in front of the custom-made Music Gate. Elvis had the gate made for Graceland by Doors, Inc. of Memphis in 1957.

Bettmann Archive

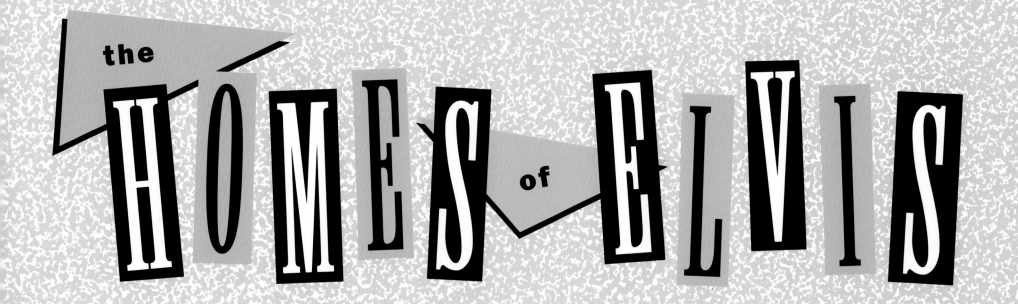

the HOMES of ELVIS

306 Old Saltillo Road, East Tupelo, Mississippi—The house where Elvis was born. Two-room wood-frame house built by Vernon Presley with $180 worth of lumber. The Presleys moved out in 1940. Was designated a state historical site by the Mississippi State Department of Archives on January 8, 1978.

Reese Street, Tupelo, Mississippi—House of Vester and Clettes Presley where Vernon, Gladys, and Elvis stayed briefly in the early 1940s.

Kelly Street, Tupelo, Mississippi—Home of the Presleys in 1942.

Berry Street, Tupelo, Mississippi—Moved in August, 1945. A $2,000 house that Vernon bought with $200 down and $30 monthly payments to Orville Bean. Vernon was forced to sell the house in 1946 because he could not keep up with the payments.

510 Maple Street, South Tupelo, Mississippi—The home of Gladys's cousin Frank Richards and his wife, Leona, where the Presleys stayed briefly.

1010 North Green Street, Tupelo, Mississippi—The last address of the Presleys in Tupelo. A four-room house in the Shakerag section of Tupelo.

572 Poplar Avenue, Memphis, Tennessee—First Memphis home of Elvis. A crowded boarding house that the Presleys shared with fifteen other families. The family lived in a single room on the ground floor.

185 Winchester Street, Memphis, Tennessee—Lauderdale Courts low-income housing project. The Presleys lived there from September, 1949 to January, 1953, when they were evicted because they were making too much money to qualify for low-income housing. Their total family income at the time was $40 per week.

398 Cypress Street, Memphis, Tennessee—Apartment house where the Presleys lived from January, 1953 to April, 1953. Monthly rent was $50.

462 Alabama Street, Memphis, Tennessee—The Presleys lived here from April, 1953 to November, 1954. This is where Elvis lived when he made his first recording at the Memphis Recording Service.

2414 Lamar Avenue, Memphis, Tennessee—The house where Elvis lived during the early part of his professional singing career, when he was recording for Sun Records. The Presleys lived here from late 1954 to mid 1955. The house is now a nursery school.

PRESLEY

1414 Getwell Street, Memphis, Tennessee—The first house Elvis rented after he was starting to enjoy some success from his singing career. The Presleys lived here from mid 1955 to May 1956.

1034 Audubon Drive, Memphis, Tennessee—A single-story, three-bedroom, ranch-style house in a wealthy suburban Memphis neighborhood that Elvis bought for $40,000 in April, 1956. The Presleys moved when the neighbors complained about fans constantly surrounding the house.

3764 Elvis Presley Boulevard, Memphis, Tennessee—Better known as Graceland. The one house that Elvis considered his true home. Elvis lived here from March, 1957 until his death.

906 Oak Hill Drive, Killeen, Texas—Four-bedroom house that Elvis rented in May, 1958 for Gladys, Vernon, Minnie Mae (Elvis's grandmother), and himself while he was stationed at Fort Hood, Texas.

Goethestrasse 14, Bad Nauheim, West Germany—Home of Elvis, Vernon, and Minnie Mae from Mid 1958 to 1959, while Elvis was stationed in West Germany in the Army.

565 Perugia Way, Bel Air, California—Designed by Frank Lloyd Wright and once owned by the Shah of Iran, Elvis rented this house from 1960 to 1963 and stayed there when he was filming his movies in Hollywood.

1059 Bellagio Road, Bel Air, California—Huge house with a bowling alley in the basement that Elvis rented briefly in 1965.

845 Chino Canyon Road, Palm Springs, California—A single-story, fifteen-room Spanish house that Elvis built in 1965. Primarily a vacation house for Presley. The house was eventually sold after Presley's death.

10550 Rocco Place, Bel Air, California—Located in Stone Canyon, a ranch-style house that Elvis rented from late 1965 to May, 1967.

1174 Hillcrest, Los Angeles, California—A three-bedroom house bought by Elvis in May, 1967 for $400,000. He lived there until late 1967.

144 Monovale, Los Angeles, California—A two-story house that Elvis bought in 1967 for $400,000. This house became his primary Los Angeles residence until he and Priscilla divorced. Priscilla continued to live there after the divorce. Elvis sold the house in 1975 to Telly Savalas.

Opposite page, top: The blue-and-gold color scheme of the dining room at Graceland is really quite subdued compared to the red decor the room sported at the time Elvis died. Just before Graceland was opened to the public, the dining room was restored to the pre-1974 decor. Opposite page, bottom: A view through the living room to the music room, which housed Elvis's gold piano. This room was built by Graceland's original owners, Dr. and Mrs. Moore, for their daughter, a harpist for the Memphis Symphony Orchestra. Right: the King poses in front of his $18,000 Rolls Royce in the driveway of Graceland on December 21, 1960. His cars and his home were Elvis's most valued possessions.

Wide World Photos

Elvis died in Graceland on August 16, 1977, and was buried on the grounds between his mother and father in the meditation garden. The ownership of Graceland and the Presley estate was put into a trust fund for Lisa Marie until she is twenty-five years of age. Elvis's former wife, Priscilla Presley, who handles her daughter's trust fund, opened Graceland to the public as a museum on June 7, 1982.

In the opening ceremonies, Graceland executive director Jack Soden said, "The Presley family felt the mansion, Graceland herself, is the best place for a museum about Elvis. This place is Elvis. You feel him here, and you always will. Elvis made history here. Graceland remains a monument to him and the musical era he created."

Today, visitors can tour the living room, dining room, music room, television room, pool room, jungle room, trophy room, and racquetball court, as well as see part of Elvis's automobile collection and tour through his jet, the *Lisa Marie*, which is on display across the street from the mansion.

Nearly 2,500 people visit Graceland every day, making it the second-most-visited private home after the White House. The tour begins with the purchase of a ticket across the street from the house at what amounts to an Elvis Presley strip mall. From there, visitors get on a bus that takes them across Elvis Presley Boulevard, through the Music Gate, and up the winding driveway to the house.

The first rooms to be seen inside Graceland are the living room and the dining room. These are perhaps the most ordinary rooms in the house, yet they are still flamboyant by most people's decorating standards. Crystal chandeliers hang over a mirrored dining room table. The windows are covered with heavy blue drapes featuring gold trim. In the living room stained glass peacocks stand watch over the furnishings. The rugs and furniture are pure white. It is in these two rooms that Elvis did most of his formal entertaining.

Blue, white, and gold were the dominant colors of Graceland's decor during the Priscilla years. After the divorce, however, when Elvis was living with former Miss Tennessee Linda Thompson, the general color scheme of the house was changed to red. There were red rugs, red drapes, and red upholstered furniture. Before opening Graceland to the public, however, Priscilla revised the decor once again so that the house looked much the way it had when she was living there.

Elvis and girlfriend Linda Thompson used more than 400 yards (360 m) of red print fabric to create the pleated tent look of the pool room. This is one of the few rooms in the house to retain the post-1974 red look.

The Jungle Room is the most extreme of all the rooms in Graceland. It was also Elvis's favorite room and the only room he designed on his own. One day Elvis was watching television when he saw a commercial for Donald's Furniture. The store featured a large selection of Polynesian-style furniture. Elvis made arrangements to have the store opened for him after midnight that night. Elvis went through the store and picked out furniture, carpeting and decorative touches for the entire den. He bought rough-cut varnished cypress tables, Tiki god lamps, couches with rabbit fur cushions and gargoyle arms, and seven-foot pine "thrones" that were so immense that a window had to be removed in order to get them in the house. The floors and ceiling of the Jungle Room are covered in thick green shag carpeting. The entire room is anchored by a stone waterfall.

Next, the tour goes outside to the carport where several of Elvis's most famous automobiles are on display. There is the 1955 pink Fleetwood Cadillac he bought for his mother, two Stutz Blackhawks, the pink Jeep from *Blue Hawaii,* a black Ferrari, a Dune Buggy, two golf carts, and a black Harley-Davidson motorcycle. (Elvis's famous gold Cadillac is on display at the Country Music Hall of Fame in Nashville, Tennessee.) While he was alive, Elvis liked to keep all of his cars lined up in the driveway in front of Graceland with the keys in them, ready to go at any moment.

The Trophy Room is one of the extra rooms Elvis added to the original house. This 40-foot-long (12m) room, which was built over the back patio, was originally a playroom. Elvis eventually used it for storing his 63 gold singles, 26 platinum records, and the other memorabilia he collected over the years. There are photo albums from his movies, the three Grammy Awards he won for his gospel album *How Great Thou Art,* a ceramic hound dog, a collection of his stage costumes, framed letters from Herbert Hoover, Lyndon Johnson, and Richard Nixon, Elvis's collection of law-enforcement badges, a trophy for being named one of America's outstanding young men by the Jaycees, and much more.

Finally, there is the racquetball court. Reportedly, on the night he died, Elvis played racquetball for several hours and then sat by himself playing the piano just outside the court. He was preparing to begin a new tour the very next day.

Visitors to Graceland are restricted from the upstairs of Graceland. This floor includes the master bedroom, Lisa Marie's room, and the bathroom where Elvis died. Elvis's Aunt Delta Mae Presley still lives upstairs in Graceland, where she worked for many years

Next on the Graceland tour is the music room, complete with a gold concert grand piano. This room is still decorated in the red motif prevalent during the Thompson years. Biographer Albert Goldman wrote that walking into this room was like walking into a giant heart. It is here that Elvis worked out the arrangements to most of his songs. The music room was also the place where Elvis chose to spend his relaxation time, passing hours sitting at the piano playing and singing in order to unwind.

Past the kitchen and down the staircase, with mirrors on the walls and ceiling, are the television room and the pool room. Inspired by LBJ in the White House, Elvis had three televisions installed on a wall in the television room, so he could watch several shows at one time. Elvis was known to shoot out the tube of a television set with a pistol if he saw something he didn't like. He shot out the image of Robert Goulet on several occasions. Writ large on the wall in the television room are the letters TCB and a lightning-bolt insignia. TCB stands for "Taking Care of Business," which was Elvis's motto.

The walls and ceiling of the pool room are covered with more than 400 yards (360m) of pleated red cotton fabric, making this room look even more like the inside of a heart than the music room. Also in the pool room are a working jukebox and a home-movie projector.

Wide World Photos

© Mark Gibson

as a housekeeper. Part of Elvis's will stipulated that if any of his family members wished to continue living at Graceland after his death, they could do so.

On the surface, Graceland may seem tacky and ill-conceived, the product of a self-indulgent personality. Elvis Presley's life took many bizarre turns while he was living there, and these are reflected in the decor of the place. But Graceland is a house that is true to its owner. It represents the flash, image, and extremes that made Elvis Presley the King of rock and roll. While it was Elvis's home, it was also his prison. His fame was so extreme that for the majority of his adult life he was unable to comfortably go out in public. As a result, Graceland became his world. Only there was he in control of his surroundings, which he could manipulate and change in any way that he wanted.

It is interesting to note that on the night that Elvis died, the lights in the meditation garden, where he would eventually be buried, mysteriously went off.

Above: Fans anxiously wait for a chance to get into the public viewing of Elvis's body held the day after his death. Left: Elvis's grave at Meditation Garden.

"Elvis Presley was a weapon of the American psychological war aimed at inflicting a part of the population with a new philosophical outlook of inhumanity..."

— *Youth World* (an East German Communist newspaper)

chapter five

ELVIS
IN THE ARMY

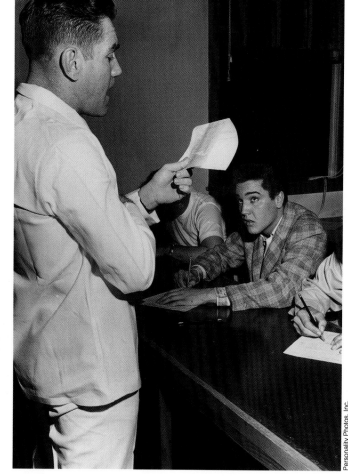

Personality Photos, Inc.

Elvis fills out his induction papers at Fort Chaffee, Arkansas. He would soon be assigned the serial number 53310761.

By December of 1957, Elvis Presley was twenty-three years old, healthy, rich, and more famous than he could have ever dreamed. In addition, he was quickly becoming one of Hollywood's major stars. His movie debut, *Love Me Tender* (November, 1956), although panned by critics, was an instant box office smash. He quickly followed up that success with *Loving You* (July, 1957), the first film that was an Elvis Presley vehicle from start to finish, and then *Jailhouse Rock* (October, 1957), both of which were also huge box office successes. He was scheduled to begin his fourth film, *King Creole,* on January 20, 1958. *King Creole* was to be directed by *Casablanca* director Michael Curtiz. Elvis was hoping that this picture would not only be a financial success, but would also legitimize his film career. In less than one year of movie making, Elvis Presley had gone from being the country's number one recording artist to being one of its most bankable movie stars.

He and his family had recently moved into Graceland and were preparing to spend their first Christmas in their Memphis "dream home." Life could not have been better for Elvis Presley. Everything he touched turned to gold. It was as if nothing could get in his way. That is, until December 10, 1957, when Elvis received a letter from the Memphis Draft Board notifying him that he was up for the next military draft. Army, Navy, and Air Force recruiters immediately called to offer him special enlistment opportunities if he signed up before being drafted. The Navy even offered to form an "Elvis Presley Company" that would include soldiers from the Memphis area.

Elvis declined all the enlistment offers and decided to take his chances with the draft. On December 19, nine days after he received his initial draft notification, Elvis got final word from the Memphis Draft Board; he was to report for induction into the Army on January 20, 1958, the very same day he was scheduled to start filming *King Creole.*

Things suddenly got very quiet around Graceland. Elvis was sure that after two years in the Army and being out of the public eye his career would be over. The first Christmas at Graceland, to which Elvis had so looked forward, had instead turned into an event that bordered on the surreal. Christmas was Elvis's favorite holiday, so he tried to act as if nothing unusual was going on. He bought a huge white Christmas tree and decorated it with hundreds of lights and bright red ornaments. He also bought thousands of dollars of fireworks to shoot off on Christmas Eve. He gave each of his employees a $1,000 bill and bought hundreds of presents for his family and friends.

According to those present, however, Elvis was very preoccupied with his military induction. At one moment he would be laughing and having a good time and the next he would blankly stare off into the distance or burst out in a sudden fit of ill temper. In a strange test of loyalty, he would leave $1,000 dollar bills lying around his room and then arrange it so that each of his guests was left alone in the room with the money. It was as if Elvis felt his career was about to take a plunge and he needed to find out just who he could trust.

Hal Wallis and Paramount were equally distressed about Elvis being drafted. They had already invested $350,000 in *King Creole* and were now faced with the possibility of shelving the project, if not canceling it entirely. Wallis and Colonel Parker contacted the Memphis Draft Board, requesting a deferment until March 20, when shooting of the film would be complete. The draft board had already been deluged by letters from angry fans who saw the conscription as a government attempt to sabotage Elvis's career. They argued that Elvis Presley was a national treasure and therefore should be exempt from the draft. The president himself even received letters regarding the "Elvis Presley draft situation." In order to ebb the tide of criticism, the draft board agreed to grant Elvis a sixty-day deferment. Of

Elvis was extremely worried about being out of the public eye for two long years. Just as his career was reaching its pinnacle, it was quickly halted by a notice from the U.S. Army. On the day he was inducted, his income dropped to $78 a month.

Personality Photos, Inc.

star and the first threat to Elvis's reign as the "King of rock and roll." Presley knew his fans were dedicated, but two years seemed like an awfully long time to wait.

Colonel Parker, however, knew better. Elvis had plenty of recorded material that had not yet been released, as well as a lot of material recorded at Sun that was still to be re-released. If RCA spaced out the releases properly, there would be more than enough to keep Elvis on charts while he was in the Army. *Jailhouse Rock* was still packing theaters across the country and *King Creole* was scheduled to be released in July. The very fact that this would be Presley's last picture until at least 1960 assured its box office success.

Colonel Parker quickly put his promotional machine in motion. If anything, Elvis joining the Army was a public-relations boon. He could now be seen as a patriotic young man who would willingly serve his country with great pride. Nearly everybody thought that Elvis would request the Special Services Branch of the Army. Indeed, the Army hierarchy was hoping that that would be the case. In the Special Services, Elvis could sing his way through his service as well as appear on print and television commercials to help the Army boost enlistment.

Opposite page: "Hair today, gone tomorrow," is what Elvis told reporters when his hair was shorn by barber James B. Peterson of Guns, Oklahoma.

Left: Elvis kisses Gladys after he passes his Army physical. Below: Elvis being plucked and probed during the induction procedures at Fort Chaffee, Arkansas.

course, as soon as the deferment was granted, those who didn't like Presley complained that he was receiving special treatment.

Elvis went to Hollywood in January to film *King Creole* as planned. The film was completed in mid-March and Elvis returned to Memphis. On March 24, 1958, Elvis reported to Local Draft Board 86 to begin his service in the United States Army. The enlistment process turned into a media circus, instigated no doubt by Colonel Parker. Dozens of reporters and photographers as well as a film crew were there to document the historic event. Flash bulbs popped constantly as Elvis went from station to station. He was asked questions, examined, tested, issued his equipment, and designated his serial number—53310761. He then boarded a bus for Fort Chaffee, Arkansas, to continue the processing.

Newspapers immediately announced the downfall of Elvis Presley. They predicted that two years out of the limelight was too much for even Elvis to overcome. Suddenly, his income was cut from $400,000 to $78 a month. Although Elvis tried to take everything in stride, deep down he was afraid for his career. Sun Records' newest artist, Jerry Lee Lewis, was emerging as a major

At Parker's insistence, however, Elvis turned down Special Services and announced that he did not want any special treatment. Parker knew that if Elvis went through basic training, carried his own gear and rifle, marched, and went on guard duty, all just like a normal soldier, that it would help his public image. The sight of Private Elvis Presley with his hair shorn, proudly wearing his olive drabs, would make any disgruntled parent think twice about his effect on their children.

Instead of Special Services, Elvis was assigned to A Company, Second Medium Tank Battalion, Second Armored Division. After four days of processing at Fort Chaffee, Elvis was shipped to Fort Hood, Texas, to begin basic training. According to Elvis, he was kidded and chided quite a bit by his fellow soldiers at the beginning of boot camp; however, once they saw that he didn't expect to be treated any differently and that he was just another grunt, they soon grew to like him.

While he was stationed at Fort Hood, the Army allowed Elvis to live off base with his parents and his grandmother. Such a practice was not unusual for a soldier with a dependent family.

The Presleys originally lived in a trailer, but later moved into a four-bedroom house at 906 Oak Hill Drive in Killeen, Texas.

While Elvis was in the middle of basic training, Gladys grew increasingly ill. She tried to hide her illness from her family until Vernon came home one day and found her collapsed on the kitchen floor. After seeing a doctor, it was agreed that Gladys would go back to Memphis and check into a hospital for tests.

Gladys had not been very healthy for some time now. She had always dreamed of the best for Elvis and wanted his singing career to take off. However, as his popularity grew, he was home less and less, and Gladys sank into depression. To deal with her loneliness and fears, Gladys drank heavily while Elvis was away, and even began taking diet pills in order to lose weight. Gladys was always afraid she was "not good enough" to enjoy her son's newfound fame. She was a country girl at heart and preferred a simple lifestyle. But after Elvis became famous, their life was anything but simple. And so, as her son's career took off, Gladys's physical and mental health declined.

Gladys Presley was admitted to the Methodist Hospital in Memphis where she was diagnosed as having acute hepatitis, brought on by a liver ailment. Her health grew worse and Elvis was granted a leave in order to be with her. In *I Called Him Babe*, Elvis's nurse, Marion Cocke, wrote that Elvis told her that when he visited his mother in the hospital, the last thing she said to him was: "Son, when you get here tomorrow, I want you to see that all

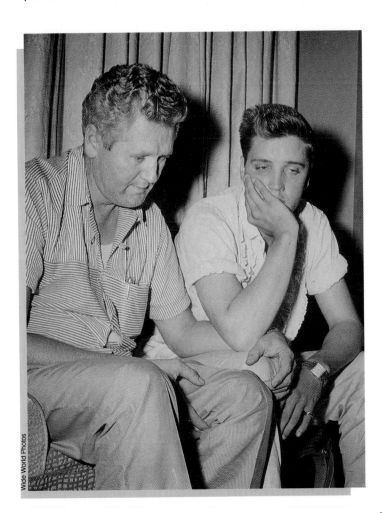

Above: Vernon, Gladys, and Elvis on their way to a preview of *King Creole* in Memphis on June 6, 1958, during Elvis's first leave from the Army. Left: Vernon and Elvis console each other at 3:15 a.m., August 14, 1958, just after Gladys's death.

Opposite page: Elvis approached Army life like a normal soldier and asked for no special treatment. Here he dishes himself some salad from the "chow line" at the beginning of eight weeks of basic training at Fort Hood, Texas.

Wide World Photos

Private Elvis Presley looks back as he carries his duffle bag aboard the transport that will take him to West Germany.

these flowers are given to other patients." Gladys Love Smith Presley died at 3:00 a.m. on August 14, 1958 of a heart attack brought on by the hepatitis. She was forty-six years old.

Elvis was devastated by his mother's death. She was the most important person in his life. He had always maintained that everything he did, he did for her. She was the only person he could really talk to and truly trust.

Gladys Presley was buried a few days later at the Forest Hill Cemetery in Memphis, a few blocks away from Graceland. Her favorite gospel group, the Blackwood Brothers, sang "Rock of Ages" and "Precious Memories" at the funeral. Crowds of fans

and photographers intruded on the funeral as Elvis mourned his mother's death. The King was so overtaken by grief that he openly sobbed and nearly collapsed several times during the service.

Many years later, after Elvis's death, Gladys's body was moved along with her son's to the meditation gardens at Graceland. Her tombstone reads:

GLADYS SMITH PRESLEY
APRIL 25, 1912—AUGUST 14, 1958
BELOVED WIFE OF VERNON PRESLEY
AND MOTHER OF ELVIS PRESLEY
SHE WAS THE SUNSHINE OF OUR HOME

In September, 1958, Elvis Presley and the 1,400 other members of his company boarded a train to New York, where they were to have a brief layover before being shipped off to West Germany, where Elvis would finish out the final year and a half of his service. As had become commonplace, the train was greeted by throngs of fans, reporters, and photographers. An Army band played "Hound Dog" and a press conference was held. This was the country's first real glimpse of Elvis Presley the soldier. He was fit, tan, and healthy-looking with his hair cut short and bleached back to its natural blond from the hot Texas sun.

On September 22, Elvis and his fellow soldiers were shipped out of the Brooklyn Navy Yards aboard the USS *General Randall*, bound for Bremerhaven, West Germany. On the eve of their departure, Elvis was promoted to Private First Class.

Unbeknownst to Elvis, he was nearly as popular in West Germany as in the United States. In fact, he had looked forward to his foreign service to provide a break from the media scrutiny and fan obsession. Peace and quiet were not to be found, however. Nearly 2,000 screaming German fans greeted the USS *General Randall* when it docked in Bremerhaven on October 1. A near riot

Elvis poses in front of the Company "D" Army barracks in Friedberg, West Germany on October 9, 1958.

Wide World Photos

Bettmann Archive

Dubbed by the press "The girl he left behind," Priscilla Beaulieu writes a letter to Elvis on March 1, 1960. Already back in the States, Elvis would be officially released from the Army in two days.

his country. One of his sergeants gave Elvis and some other soldiers the amphetamine Dexedrine to help them stay awake at night while on guard duty. Over the years, Elvis developed a vicious dependence on a vast array of prescription medicine; addictions that would eventually contribute to his early death.

Elvis behaved just like any other soldier when he was on duty. He marched, he carried a gun, and he pulled KP and guard duty. At night, however, he returned to his home in Bad Nauheim, where he invited a vast array of family, friends, and fellow soldiers over practically every night. The parties consisted mostly of a number of people just hanging out, talking, with the occasional jam session taking place. On one such night late in 1959, one of Elvis's Army buddies, U.S. Airman Currie Grant, brought over a young girl named Priscilla Beaulieu.

Born on May 25, 1945, Priscilla was the daughter of Navy lieutenant James Wagner and his wife, Ann. Wagner, however, was killed in a plane crash just six months after Priscilla's birth. Priscilla's mother married another military man, Joseph Beaulieu, two years later. Soon after the wedding, Beaulieu officially adopted Priscilla. When Priscilla met Elvis, Joseph Beaulieu was a Captain in the 1405 Support Squadron at the Wiesbaden Air Force Base in West Germany.

Elvis immediately took to the five-foot-three, blue-eyed beauty, and the two began dating regularly during the last few months of Elvis's service. Usually, Elvis would send a driver over to pick Priscilla up and bring her to his house. Captain Beaulieu, however, was very concerned about the situation, particularly because Priscilla was only fourteen years old at the time, so he told Elvis that if he wanted to see Priscilla he had to come pick her up and bring her home himself.

Priscilla, or "Cilla," as Elvis called her, soon became a fixture at the house at Bad Nauheim, as well as the object of Elvis's obsessions. Elvis had been involved with quite a few women over the past few years; however, none of them exuded the innocence, purity, beauty, and unbridled honesty that Elvis saw in the 14-year-old Priscilla Beaulieu. Almost from the moment he met her, Elvis told his friends and family that she was the woman for him. Priscilla filled the role of the woman in Elvis's life that had recently been vacated with the death of his mother. Elvis constantly commented on how much Gladys would have loved Priscilla and that she must be looking after him from heaven, otherwise he never would have met Priscilla.

ensued when they saw Elvis walk in line with the rest of the troops, carrying his own duffle bag. The troops took a train to Weisbaden, where they would be replacements in the Fourth Armored Division.

As in Texas, Elvis was permitted to live off base with his family. He rented a modest four-bedroom, two-story house in Bad Nauheim where he lived with Vernon, his grandmother Minnie Mae (whom he affectionately nicknamed "Dodger"), as well as a few members of the Memphis Mafia, including Red West and Earl Greenwood.

Elvis was assigned duty as a jeep driver—the perfect assignment for a man who loved cars as much as he did. According to fellow soldiers, he spent hours cleaning, polishing, and maintaining his jeep and was one of only five who got a perfect rating in an inspection of more than three hundred jeeps and other vehicles. On June 14, he was rewarded for his diligence by being promoted to Corporal.

In November, the entire 32nd Tank Battalion was sent on maneuvers close to the Czechoslovakian border. Elvis and his fellow soldiers spent several weeks engaged in round-the-clock exercises, getting what little sleep they were allowed lying on the ground in the cold German nights. Ironically, Elvis's first exposure to drugs occurred during these maneuvers while in the service of

Personality Photos, Inc.

Back home at last, Sergeant Presley steps off a private rail car in Memphis on March 7, 1960. Elvis briefly greeted his fans then immediately headed for Graceland.

Wide World Photos

Priscilla's age was no doubt part of the attraction. Perhaps because Elvis had such little control over his runaway fame and the direction of his career, he exercised an almost dictatorial control over his home life. He surrounded himself with friends and bodyguards who were always at his beck and call. Priscilla was young, impressionable, and easily molded into Elvis's ideal of the perfect woman. He directed her to dye her hair jet black (just like his), pile it up in a high bouffant, and wear heavy, dark eye make-up. The "Priscilla Presley look" that she made famous in the 1960s was developed completely by Elvis himself.

For Priscilla, meeting Elvis Presley was a dream come true. Like millions of other teenagers, she had bought all of Presley's records and followed his career closely in the fan magazines. When Elvis was shipped to Germany, Priscilla became excited about just being in the same country as Elvis. She had no idea she would ever even meet Elvis Presley, let alone become the object of his affections. Just as she became used to the idea that she was dating Elvis Presley, however, it seemed as if the whole romance would come to an abrupt end. Only a few months after they met, Elvis's tour of duty with the Army was over.

Priscilla waved a tearful goodbye to Elvis as he boarded the plane leaving Germany for the United States. Elvis searched her out of the large crowd just before he got on the plane and waved to her. In the press, she became known as "the girl he left behind." When questioned at a press conference back in the states, Elvis denied that any type of romance was going on between him and Priscilla. He simply described her as a young girl he had met and befriended, that it was nothing special.

Well before he came home, America had already begun preparing for the return of Elvis Presley. Nobody had taken over Presley's reign during his absence. Jerry Lee Lewis had made a push, but was then brought down by the scandal surrounding his marriage to his thirteen-year-old cousin. Buddy Holly, Richie Valens, and the Big Bopper had all enjoyed skyrocketing success in rock and roll; however, their lives were tragically cut short in a plane crash in 1959. Even though he had spent two years without making a record or a public appearance, Elvis Presley still ruled the record charts and the radio. *Jailhouse Rock* was re-released and pulled in $2 million in the first few weeks of its second run.

Elvis was coming home to the United States as an even bigger star than when he had left. And just as Colonel Parker had predicted, Elvis Presley was now viewed as a respected star. He was no longer perceived as a threat to teenage morals and family values by church and parent groups. Instead of being a dangerous rebel, Elvis had become an all-American boy who had realized a rags-to-riches dream. The King was finally accepted by the establishment.

Upon his return, the Mississippi State Legislature passed a resolution stating that Elvis Presley had become "a legend and an inspiration to tens of millions of Americans and hence reaffirms a historic American ideal that success in our nation can still be attained through individual initiative, hard work and abiding faith in one's self and in the Creator."

Elvis returned to Memphis in late February, 1960 and hung up his Army uniform for good. (Twenty years later, the Presley estate lent it to the makers of the docudrama *This is Elvis* to be worn by actor David Scott. The estate trustees were so pleased with Scott's portrayal of Elvis that they gave him the uniform.) After spending a few weeks relaxing at Graceland, Elvis headed for

Bettmann Archive

Priscilla created quite a stir at the airport when she waved goodbye to Elvis as he left Germany at the end of his 18-month tour of duty.

Miami Beach, where he was to tape a television special with Frank Sinatra. "Welcome Home, Elvis," which was taped on March 26 and aired on May 12, 1960, was the final Frank Sinatra-Timex TV special of the season. The show was recorded before a live audience at the Grand Ballroom of the Miami Beach Fontainbleau Hotel. Elvis was paid $125,000 for his six-minute appearance.

It is indicative of Presley's newfound acceptance that Sinatra would even allow Presley to appear on his show, let alone stage a big welcome-home celebration. Just three years earlier, Sinatra had said of Elvis and his music: "His kind of music is deplorable, a rancid-smelling aphrodisiac . . . [rock and roll] is the most brutal, ugly, degenerate, vicious form of expression it has been my displeasure to hear. It fosters almost totally negative and destructive reactions in young people. It smells phony and false. It is sung, played, and written for the most part by cretinous goons,

and by means of its almost imbecilic reiterations and sly, lewd—in plain fact, dirty—lyrics, it manages to be the martial music of every side-burned delinquent on the face of the earth."

"Welcome Home, Elvis" opened with the entire cast—which included Sammy Davis Jr., Peter Lawford, Joey Bishop, Nancy Sinatra, Frank Sinatra, and Elvis—singing "It's Nice to Go Traveling." Elvis appeared later in the show to sing "Fame and Fortune" and "Stuck On You," the two sides of his soon-to-be-released single, the first since his release from the Army. At the end of the show, Elvis sang a duet with Frank Sinatra, in which Elvis sang Sinatra's hit "Witchcraft" and Sinatra sang "Love Me Tender."

Elvis Presley was back, and bigger than ever. And now his audience was not limited just to the under-twenty crowd. His appearance with Sinatra gave him immediate credibility with a whole new audience. One of the main reasons the Colonel signed him on for the special was to appeal to this older crowd. Elvis wore a tuxedo for the special and appeared alone, without his band. Even his stage movements were a toned-down version of the infamous gyrations that had previously excited teenage fans and outraged their parents. The final coup came when Elvis sang the duet of "Love Me Tender"/"Witchcraft" with Frank Sinatra. Here were the two singing sex symbols of their respective generations on stage together—trading off verses, singing each other's songs, and ending together in perfect harmony. Unfortunately, this triumph proved to be Elvis Presley's last television appearance and his second-to-last public performance for eight years.

Interestingly, the costar of *G.I. Blues*, Elvis's first film after the Army, was Juliet Prowse, Frank Sinatra's fiancée at the time. While shooting the film, Elvis reportedly had an affair with Prowse. When Sinatra found out about the affair, he sent a few of his "associates" over to suggest to Elvis that he end the affair immediately. Elvis also had an affair with Sinatra's daughter, Nancy, with whom he would later star with in *Speedway* (1968). Frank, however, was far less concerned about that affair. Nancy and Elvis remained good friends long after their affair ended. In fact, it was Nancy who threw Priscilla her baby shower.

Immediately following the show, Elvis headed for Nashville for a marathon recording session that lasted twelve hours and yielded twelve songs. Orders for his first single, "Stuck On You"/ "Fame and Fortune" (RCA-47-7740) exceeded one million copies before the songs were even recorded. The songs from this session were put together on an album entitled *Elvis is Back.*

Just two weeks after he arrived home to Graceland, Elvis headed for Miami Beach, where he taped a television special with Frank Sinatra. Here, Elvis and Frank sing a duet, with Elvis singing "Witchcraft" and Frank singing "Love Me Tender".

Motion Picture & TV Archives

Personality Photos, Inc.

Elvis takes a bite of his welcome-home cake in the yard at Graceland. His home-coming was bitter-sweet, for Graceland would never be the same without the pres-ence of his mother.

Personality Photos, Inc.

"That boy can charm the birds right out of the trees."

—Richard Egan, Elvis's co-star
in *Love Me Tender*

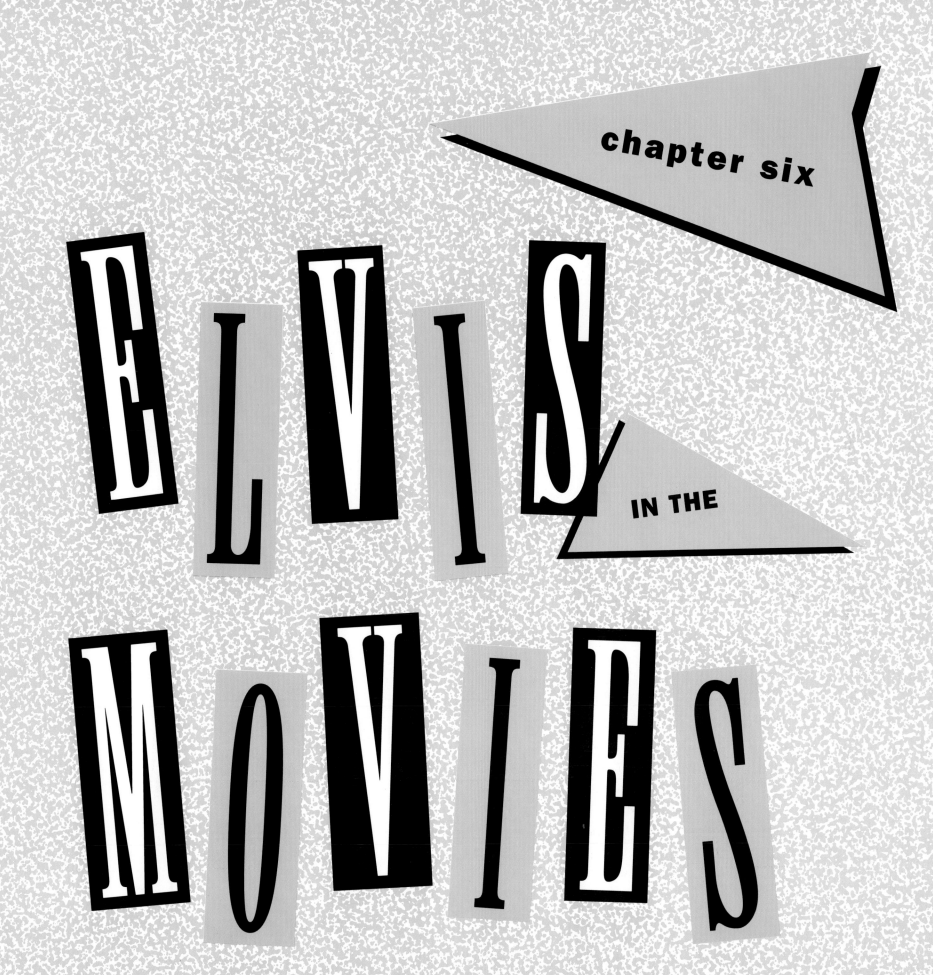

chapter six

ELVIS, IN THE MOVIES

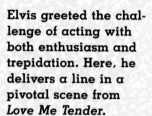

Elvis greeted the challenge of acting with both enthusiasm and trepidation. Here, he delivers a line in a pivotal scene from *Love Me Tender.*

Elvis greeted the challenge of acting with both enthusiasm and trepidation. Here, he delivers a line in a pivotal scene from *Love Me Tender.*

Elvis Presley had loved the movies ever since he was a young boy growing up in Memphis. Going to the movies was an escape from the poverty Elvis saw in his everyday life. For a few pennies, he could thrust himself into the middle of a Western gun battle, or enjoy the plush elegance of an aristocratic mansion. One of Elvis's first jobs was as an usher at the Loew's State Theatre in Memphis, and even as his music was receiving its first air play on Memphis radio, Elvis escaped to the movies rather than experience the anxiety of listening to his own voice broadcast over the airwaves.

When Elvis became so famous that he could no longer venture outside in daylight, he used to gather up his friends and family and take them to the Memphian Theater, which he would rent from midnight to five in the morning. Among his favorite films were *Wuthering Heights, Rebel Without a Cause, Letter from an Unknown Woman, Miracle on 34th Street, It's a Wonderful Life, Mr. Skeffington, Dr. Strangelove,* and *The Godfather.*

So it was with a great deal of excitement that Elvis went out to Hollywood to make his first motion picture. Elvis had signed a three-picture deal with producer Hal Wallis and Paramount pictures; however, since none of these projects was yet ready for filming, Elvis made his first movie with Twentieth-Century Fox.

(Elvis never signed an exclusive contract with any one studio.)

In August, 1956, Elvis left his new home at Graceland and headed for Hollywood to begin work on *The Reno Brothers,* a Western starring veteran actors Richard Egan and Debra Paget. Elvis was determined to prove that he could act. According to all reports, he was always on time for rehearsals and filming, and was extremely polite and agreeable to the director and his co-stars. He was certainly not the prima donna, rock-and-roll rebel that the cast and crew expected. Nor did he fit in with the Hollywood scene. He very seldom went to parties and spent most of his spare time working on his lines or relaxing in his hotel room.

Principal shooting for the film began on August 23 and was completed on October 8. The picture told the story of the four Reno brothers, of which Richard Egan played the oldest and Elvis the youngest. The three older brothers go off to fight for the South in the Civil War, leaving Elvis behind to run the ranch. Word comes back that Egan has been killed. The distraught Elvis falls in love with and marries Debra Paget, who, unbeknownst to Elvis, had been engaged to Egan.

Eventually, Egan and his brothers return from the war. There is a subplot involving a stolen payroll, which pits Elvis against his own brother. Elvis wounds his brother, but then realizes he made a mistake. The film ends with Elvis being killed as he is trying to run

Personality Photos, Inc.

The first-time actor takes a break during the filming of *Love Me Tender*.

to his wounded brother to try and save his life. A second ending was filmed in which Elvis lived, but it was shelved in favor of the dramatic death scene. In order to placate fans who would be upset at seeing their hero die on screen, the producers decided to superimpose a close-up of Elvis singing *Love Me Tender* over the closing credits.

Originally, there were no plans for any songs in the film. However, during the shoot, producer David Weisbart—who went on to produce three other Presley films, *Flaming Star* (1960), *Follow That Dream* (1962), and *Kid Galahad* (1962)—realized Elvis's tremendous box office appeal and decided to add four songs and change the name of the film to *Love Me Tender* to take advantage of Presley's current hit. Although Presley was billed third in the credits, below Egan and Debra Paget, he soon became the film's true star. This was the only film on which Elvis did not receive top billing.

So with the words, "Whoa! Brett! Vance! They told us you were dead!" Elvis Presley began a film career that was to span twelve years and thirty-three pictures.

Love Me Tender opened in New York on November 15, 1956, at the Paramount Theater. A fifty-foot (15m) cut-out, covered with white paper and a big question mark, was erected above the marquee. Just before showtime, the paper was peeled off, revealing a giant picture of Elvis in Western garb holding a guitar. Crowds began gathering outside the theater at 7 o'clock that morning for the premier.

During the 1950s, the studios normally made about 200 to 300 prints of a film for major release. The pre-release demand for *Love Me Tender* was so strong that Twentieth-Century Fox ordered 550 prints instead.

The film was an immediate box office smash. Within three days, it had recouped its total production cost of $1 million. *Love Me Tender* was the first Hollywood film to earn its money back that quickly. It reached number 2 on *Variety's* list of top-grossing films, and ranked number 23 of all the films of 1956, despite the fact that it had only been in release for two months during that year. In 1957, *Love Me Tender* made the list of the top twenty money-making films along with two other Presley pictures— *Jailhouse Rock* and *Loving You.*

Elvis Presley's box office success was virtually assured the minute he signed his first movie contract. He already had an audience of millions of dedicated teenage fans. By the end of

Motion Picture & TV Archives

1956, Elvis had sold more records than any single artist in the history of recorded music. In addition, Colonel Parker had embarked on a relentless promotion campaign using hundreds of different merchandising gimmicks. Charm bracelets, shoes, pencils, pens, stuffed teddy bears and hound dogs, sweaters, slippers, hair brushes, combs, diaries—virtually anything a teenager could possibly want could be bought with Elvis Presley's name or likeness emblazoned on it. Presleymania was so strong that his rabid fans would show up at any Elvis Presley picture, no matter what the story line or the quality of the movie. All they wanted was to see Elvis's image projected larger than life across the screen and have him sing a few songs.

The critics, however, were not so easy to please. Elvis Presley's movie debut was greeted with almost universal contempt by the nation's movie writers. The most vicious attack on Presley's acting appeared in *The New York Times*: "Is it a sausage? It is certainly smooth and damp-looking, but who ever heard of a 172-pound (78kg) sausage six feet (1.8m) tall? Is it a Walt Disney goldfish? It has the same sort of big, soft, beautiful eyes and long, curly lashes, but who ever heard of a goldfish with sideburns? Is it a corpse? The face just hangs there, limp and white with its little drop-seat mouth..."

Even the most ardent fan must admit that Presley's debut in *Love Me Tender* was far from spectacular. The script, however, was just as mediocre as Presley's acting. Yet, Elvis remained unfazed,

Above: Elvis stands outside his trailer on the set of *Love Me Tender*.

Opposite page: Thousands of screaming teenagers attend the unveiling of a 40-foot (12 m) cardboard likeness of Elvis Presley outside the Paramount Theater in New York.

David Weisbart, however, saw very different reasons why both men were so popular: "So far as teenagers are concerned, Elvis is what I call a safety valve. By that I mean they scream, holler, articulate, and let go of their emotions when they see him perform. But when they watched Jimmy Dean perform they bottled their emotions and were sort of sullen and brooding. Elvis is completely outgoing, where Jimmy was the direct opposite.... Jimmy was apparently the typical confused teenager, but Elvis is something every kid would like to be—a phenomenal success without having to work for it. He's up there enjoying himself and getting millions of dollars. According to a child's logic, what could be better?"

For whatever reasons, *The James Dean Story* never got off the ground. The list of pictures for which Elvis Presley was considered in the late 1950s, '60s, and '70s is quite impressive—the Tony Curtis role in *The Defiant Ones* and opposite Burt Lancaster in *The Rainmaker,* as well as parts in *Thunder Road, In Cold Blood,* and much later, *A Star Is Born* and *Midnight Cowboy.* There is much speculation as to why all these deals fell through for Elvis, but underlying all the specific reasons is Colonel Parker. Parker ruled Presley's career with an iron hand. He was always on the lookout for ways to make Elvis (and himself) richer and more famous. Parker looked at Elvis in the movies the same way he looked at all the Presley paraphernalia he produced. It was just another way to market the "King of rock and roll." For Parker to approve a movie deal for Elvis Presley, it had to be an "Elvis Presley movie." Elvis had to have top billing and the entire film had to center on his character. Often the characters in films were one-dimensional cartoons of Elvis himself—the poor boy who makes good. Also, since Presley fans didn't seem to care what Elvis did on screen or whether the movie itself was of any quality, very little effort was expended getting good or even adequate scripts, and the movies were filmed as quickly and cheaply as possible. At the heights—or depths, depending on how you look at it—of the "Elvis Presley Movie" (1961 to 1968), Elvis made 21 pictures for an incredible average of three movies per year. It is no wonder that they lacked in substance and quality. No talent, no matter how strong, could have possibly made that many pictures in such a short amount of time and succeeded, especially lacking good scripts, good direction, good supporting casts, and even the slightest amount of artistic direction. As a studio executive once commented, "These are Elvis Presley pictures. They don't

Personality Photos, Inc.

Above: Originally called *The Reno Brothers* (note the placard), the title of Presley's first film was changed in order to capitalize on his latest hit single. Opposite page: Elvis dons some flashy Western wear while performing a song from his second film, *Loving You.*

determined to pursue an acting career. He desperately wanted to be taken seriously as an actor, yet with this and subsequent pictures, Elvis became trapped in what would become a film genre all of its own—"The Elvis Presley picture."

The possibility for appearing in better movie projects existed throughout his career. During the filming of *Love Me Tender,* producer David Weisbart, who had produced James Dean in *Rebel Without a Cause,* talked with Elvis about doing the title role in *The James Dean Story.* James Dean, one of Elvis's favorite actors, had been killed the year before and demand was hot for a story about his life. Comparisons between Dean and Presley were natural. Both of them were teen idols who exuded a strong sexuality and rebelliousness.

need titles. They could be numbered." Yet, every one of Elvis Presley's movies made money, leading producer Hal Wallis to comment that "the only sure thing in show business is an Elvis Presley picture."

What of Elvis's pre-Army acting career? The development of the Elvis Presley formula did not truly begin until Presley's post-Army years, beginning with *G. I. Blues* in 1960. His four pre-Army movies, while none of them can be considered great landmarks in film, were at least made with a modicum of effort and the desire to produce work of reasonably high quality. Presley's acting improved along with the content of each film, and by the time *King Creole* was made in 1958, it almost seemed as if Elvis Presley could have developed into a competent, serious actor.

Elvis began work on the filming of *Loving You,* his second film, in January 1957, right at the height of the box office success of *Love Me Tender.* This was the first of a total of nine films Elvis was to make for Hal Wallis at Paramount Pictures. It was also the first time Presley's fans would be able to see their idol in glorious Technicolor. Unlike *Love Me Tender,* this film was to be an Elvis Presley vehicle from start to finish. Elvis appears in virtually every scene and sings a total of seven songs, including his soon-to-be number one hit "(Let Me Be Your) Teddy Bear."

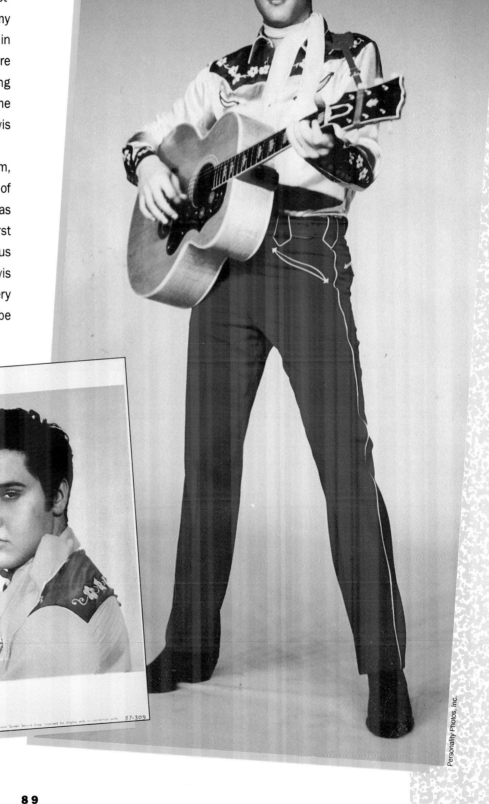

In 1959, Hart said of Elvis, "Elvis is a young man with an enormous capacity for love...but I don't think he has found his happiness. I think he is terribly lonely."

Loving You premiered on July 9, 1957 at the Strand Theater in Memphis. Elvis attended a midnight showing with his parents and his new girlfriend, Anita Wood. Again, Presley fans flocked to see it. The film reached number 7 on *Variety's* weekly list of top-grossing movies and ended the year as one of the top twenty money-making films of 1957.

Before *Loving You* was even released, Elvis had already begun filming his third movie, *Jailhouse Rock,* for MGM. This turned out to be one of Presley's most enduring films. It is fast-paced, entertaining, and contains a number of flashy, well-choreographed production numbers, including the famous "Jailhouse Rock," performed on a large set consisting of prison cells. Much of the choreography for that number was done by Presley himself. Perhaps the main reason for *Jailhouse Rock's* immediate popularity and enduring success is that it contains not only some of the best songs in any of Elvis's movies, but some of the best songs he ever recorded—"Jailhouse Rock," "(You're So Square)

Above: Elvis fends off the advances of an eager Lizabeth Scott in a scene from *Loving You*. Right: The King performs a song in *Jailhouse Rock*.

Presley's costar was the beautiful young actress Dolores Hart. This was Hart's first picture and Paramount had great hopes of her becoming a big star. As part of a publicity stunt for the film and for Hart's career, the studio had her write an article for *Photoplay* magazine entitled "What It's Like to Kiss Elvis."

During the filming of *Loving You,* Elvis began dating Hart, as he did many of his other leading ladies in subsequent films. Presley saw an honesty and sophistication in Hart that he was not used to in other women he had dated. The relationship, however, ended soon after filming was complete, and Elvis returned to Graceland. Over the next few years, Hart made nine more films in Hollywood, including *King Creole* with Presley. In 1963, she shocked everybody by quitting her movie career to become a nun. Today she is Mother Superior at the Convent of Regina Laudis in Bethlehem, Connecticut.

RCA VICTOR
PB-13892
A "New Orthophonic" High Fidelity Recording

ELVIS PRESLEY

Heartbreak Hotel b/w Jailhouse Rock

Lorraine Hansen Collection

Motion Picture & TV Archives

Elvis dances in the famous production number from *Jailhouse Rock*, parts of which he helped choreograph.

91

Always a huge fan of James Dean, Elvis got to play a troubled youth in the gritty film *King Creole*. This was his last film before going into the Army.

0216-5

45

Personality Photos, Inc.

Baby I Don't Care," and "Treat Me Nice." These songs, all written by Jerry Leiber and Mike Stoller, marked the first true blues-based rock-and-roll songs to be sung by Elvis in one of his movies.

Filming for *Jailhouse Rock* was completed on June 14, and the film premiered in Memphis on October 17, 1957. It was released nationally on November 8. Elvis received his biggest remuneration yet for a film—$250,000 plus 50 percent of the film's profits. *Jailhouse Rock* grossed $4 million in its first year. In 1960, it was re-released to coincide with Elvis's release from the Army.

Presley's final film before entering the Army was *King Creole*, his second Hal Wallis, Paramount Pictures film. *King Creole* was loosely based on the Harold Robbins novel, *A Stone For Danny Fisher*, and tells the story of a tough New Orleans kid who gets a job sweeping floors in a seedy Bourbon Street Night Club. He eventually is given a chance to sing, but becomes caught up in a conflict involving two nightclub owners (one good, one bad), the mob, and two lovely women (one basically good, but hardened by her mob boyfriend, and one good and pure who truly loves him). At the same time, he has to deal with his own inner conflicts and problems with his timid father, who has trouble relating to his streetwise son.

This is by far the grittiest and darkest of all the Elvis Presley films. Shot in black and white on a dim, shadowy soundstage, the movie examines the seedy underside of New Orleans nightlife. Elvis plays a very troubled rebel who is prone to violence and is trying to make sense of a world that belies his father's pure ideals. In future films, though Elvis continued to play rebels who make good (and who inevitably punch somebody before the last reel), his characters would be much less dark than that of Danny Fisher.

King Creole was directed by Michael Curtiz, a veteran Hollywood director who was in his prime in the 1930s and 1940s. He received four Best Director Oscar nominations between 1938 and 1942 for *Four Daughters* (1938), *Angels with Dirty Faces* (1938), *Yankee Doodle Dandy* (1942), and *Casablanca* (1942). For *Casablanca*, one of the most popular movies of all time, he finally won the Oscar.

According to reports, Curtiz did not want to work with Elvis and tried to make life very difficult for him on the set. Elvis, however, never complained, but instead worked double-time to try and please the disgruntled director. As early as preproduction, Curtiz complained that Elvis was too plump. So Elvis went on a crash diet in order to lose ten pounds in the two weeks before the

shoot. By the end of the film, it was Elvis, not Curtiz, asking for second and third takes because he was not satisfied with his performance.

The extra work paid off. *The New York Times,* which compared Elvis to a greasy sausage after his first movie, enthusiastically announced, "Elvis can act!" While Presley's performance in *King Creole* is far from perfect, it is also more than adequate and showed a vast improvement over his previous three films. The fact that he had a passable script, a competent director in Michael Curtiz, and some very talented co-stars, including Walter Matthau, who went on to win an Oscar for Best Supporting Actor for *The Fortune Cookie* (1966), and Carolyn Jones, who had just been nominated for an Academy Award for her performance in *The Bachelor Party* (1958), no doubt helped Elvis's performance as well as the picture in general. (Carolyn Jones later played Morticia in the popular television comedy *The Addams Family*.)

As with his first three films, *King Creole* was a big hit at the box office with the avid Elvis Presley fans. Interest in this film was particularly strong because it was Elvis's last project before going into the Army. No other Elvis Presley picture would hit the big screen for another two years.

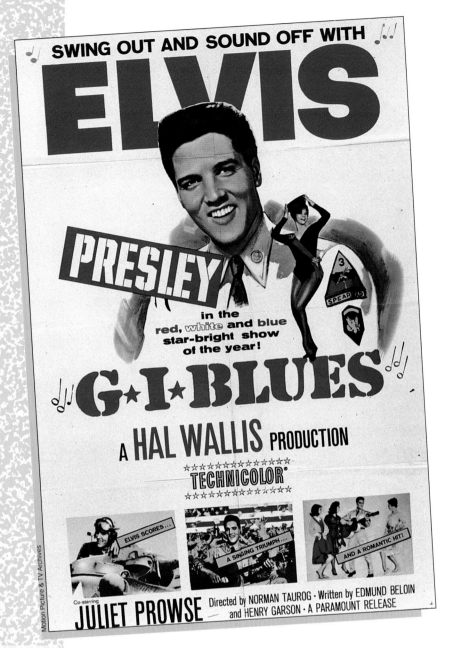

SWING OUT AND SOUND OFF WITH

ELVIS PRESLEY

in the red, white and blue star-bright show of the year!

G·I·BLUES

A HAL WALLIS PRODUCTION

TECHNICOLOR®

Co-starring JULIET PROWSE Directed by NORMAN TAUROG · Written by EDMUND BELOIN and HENRY GARSON · A PARAMOUNT RELEASE

Motion Picture & TV Archives

G. I. Blues, a loosely based fictional account of Presley's experience in the Army. In it, Elvis plays Tulsa McLean, a young, famous singer who gets drafted at the peak of his career and is sent overseas to Germany.

This film marks the beginning of the exploitation of Elvis Presley in the movies. From 1961 to 1968, he churned out twenty-one pictures, none of them very different from each other. They all stuck to basic formula of Elvis as the young handsome man down on his luck who has to endure a few far-fetched adventures and setbacks before he makes good and marries the girl. In these post-Army pictures, Elvis was pure and honest and would resort to the odd punch only when he was justifiably provoked. His characters never swore, cheated, lied, had sex, drank, or smoked. He became the young man every mother dreams for her daughter to marry. Elvis's cinematic image was a far cry from his "whirling dervish of sex" days of the 1950s.

A feature in *Life* magazine on Presley after his return from the Army stated: "The Elvis Presley everyone thinks he is, isn't. He is no longer the sneering, hip-swinging symbol of the untamed beast that resides in 17-year-old breasts." And *The Hollywood Reporter* wrote: "When they took the boy out of the country, they apparently took the country out of the boy...It is a subdued and changed Elvis Presley who has returned from the military service in Germany to star in Hal Wallis's *G. I. Blues.*"

In the 1960s, Elvis allowed control of his career to rest almost entirely in the hands of Colonel Parker and the Hollywood Studios. For example, Parker had final say over all scripts. Several directors wanted to cast Elvis in films of a more serious nature, in which he didn't play such one-dimensional characters. Director Norman Taurog, who directed several of Presley's films, went so far as to suggest that Elvis be cast as a murderer in a film. Colonel Parker, however, refused to let Elvis act in any film that made him look in any way bad. Nor would he allow him to participate in any film in which he could possibly be shown up by one of his costars, let alone play second bill to a serious actor in a serious film.

Elvis had once been an innovator in the music and entertainment industries, rebelling at every turn against the establishment; but he was now a captured pawn of the establishment. Colonel Parker and the studios were slowly changing Elvis's image from that of rock-and-roll rebel to that of a good-natured boy. In *Elvis,* Dave Marsh writes that the purpose of Elvis Presley's post-

Hal Wallis hoped to take advantage of Elvis's Army experience with *G.I. Blues,* the first film project after Presley's release from military service.

Opposite page: Elvis performs a song in *G.I. Blues.* The immense flag in the background was custom made for the film. It measures 21 by 42 feet (6 by 12 m).

The hiatus was not really that long. *King Creole* did not open nationally until July, 1958—just as the first run of *Jailhouse Rock* began to ebb—and it stayed in the theaters until nearly the end of the year. Then, towards the end of 1959, MGM rereleased *Jailhouse Rock* in order to take advantage of the excitement generated by Elvis's return from the Army.

Elvis Presley had been the most famous soldier in the Army. When he returned to civilian life in March, 1960, he was more popular than ever. Indeed, his Army service and his new all-American image had increased his audience, which finally included adults. Paramount and Hal Wallis had decided to take advantage of America's best-loved soldier long before Elvis actually left West Germany. His first picture upon returning home was

Motion Picture & TV Archives

Blue Hawaii was the first, and perhaps the best, of Presley's prototypical beach movies. Here he sings with a bevy of beach beauties.

Army films was "...not simply to diffuse and defuse the original revolutionary, anarchic spirit of Elvis Presley, but to use him as the very vehicle which keeps his audience rooted to its place in the status quo, to the concept that the only changes of importance are purely romantic ones."

Parker's machinations ensured that Elvis was tied up in movie deals four years in advance. Often Elvis would be signed to movies before he had even read the script, not that there was ever much of a script to read. Elvis could have rebelled against Parker and demanded new projects with better scripts; however, part of him remained deeply afraid of failure. At heart, Elvis was still just a poor boy from Memphis and he realized that his fame and money could disappear just as quickly as it had come. Colonel Parker had helped make him the most famous entertainer in the world, and as a result, Presley trusted Parker implicitly. At this point in his career, Elvis was unwilling to take chances of any kind, so instead he just methodically kept churning out mediocre picture after mediocre picture.

The Elvis Presley genre film hit its apex with *Blue Hawaii* in 1961. Part of the film was shot on location, after Elvis had gone to Hawaii for a benefit concert appearance (his last public performance until 1968). This film marked the first of many beach movies that Elvis would make. It costarred Angela Lansbury, who played Elvis's domineering mother, Joan Blackman—in a role originally intended for Juliet Prowse—and Jenny Maxwell. *Blue Hawaii* turned out to be Elvis's most popular movie. It was released in five hundred theaters around Christmas of 1961 and ended up grossing $4.7 million. RCA also released a soundtrack album just prior to the film's release. It was the most successful of all Elvis's soundtrack albums, selling more than five million copies and holding the number one spot on the album charts for twenty straight weeks. Nearly all of the songs on the album are highly forgettable Presley renditions of Hawaiian songs such as "Ito Fats," "Ku-U-I-Po," and "The Hawaiian Wedding Song"; however, the film did contain one huge hit that later became the classic last song in nearly all of Elvis's 1970s concert appearances—"Can't Help Falling in Love."

Quality songs such as "Can't Help Falling in Love," "Jailhouse Rock," and "(You're So Square) Baby, I Don't Care" were the exception rather than the rule in Elvis's movies. Most of the songs contracted for his films were mediocre at best. Since the signing of the RCA deal in 1956, almost all of the original material Elvis recorded was controlled by the Hill and Range Publishing Company, which had formed two subsidiary companies, Elvis Presley Music and Gladys Music. Any songwriter who wrote a song for Elvis Presley had to relinquish some of his or her royalties to Hill and Range. As a result, the best songwriters of the era refused to write songs for Presley. Hill and Range instead contracted songwriting responsibilities to their own stable of hacks, who were willing to work for little money. They gave scripts to their writers with the spaces for songs highlighted and the writers would then produce songs around the scripts. Few of the songs were memorable, and even fewer were based in rock and roll. Unfortunately for fans of Presley's music, soundtrack albums were the only source of new material from Presley for nearly eight years. RCA did, however, continually repackage and rerelease older Presley material at a rate of two or three albums per year.

Finally, by the mid-1960s, the poor quality of Elvis's movies and his music began to have an impact on their sales. His films made less money and he increasingly lost contact with the record

Wide World Photos

industry. Once again, North America was experiencing a music revolution—but this time, it was a revolution in which Elvis Presley had no part to play. The Beatles, the Rolling Stones, and the rest of the British invasion had taken America and the world by storm. Bob Dylan was writing and recording simple, poetic, and meaningful folk hits at the same time that Elvis Presley was releasing banal songs such as "If Every Day Was Like Christmas" and "Yoga is as Yoga Does."

From 1960 to 1968, Elvis did not have a single hit on the country charts and had only one hit on the rhythm and blues charts—"Devil in Disguise" (1963). He had no number one singles between "Good Luck Charm" in 1962 and "Suspicious Minds" in 1969. Elvis saw his career slowly drawing to a standstill, and by 1968, he knew it was time for a change. That year, he decided to let his movie contracts run out and go back into the studio to record his first non-soundtrack album since the early 1960s. To mark his re-entry into the music business, Elvis decided to do a primetime television special—his first public performance in eight years. It was time for a comeback.

Elvis takes a break from the filming of *Blue Hawaii* on location in Oahu. Aloft on the King's shoulders are Debra Kawamura, age 4, and Robert Kenui, age 5.

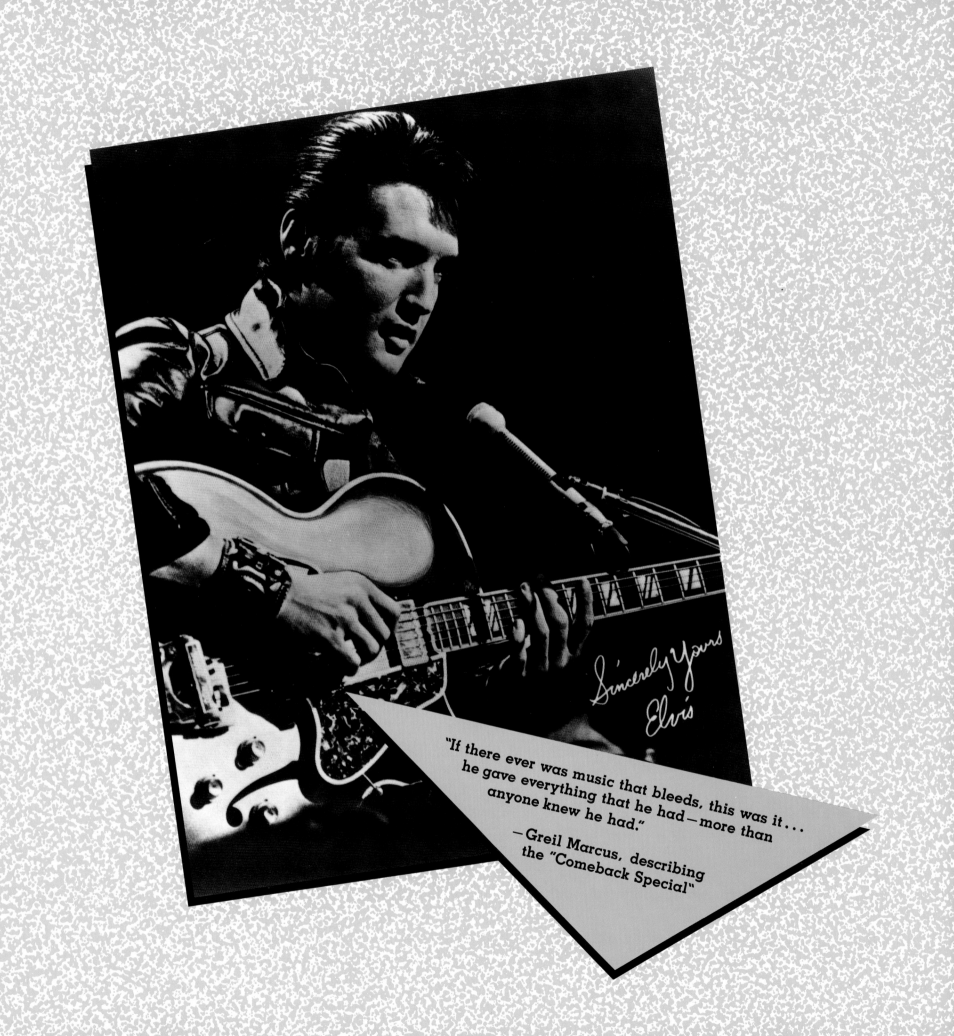

Sincerely Yours
Elvis

"If there ever was music that bleeds, this was it... he gave everything that he had—more than anyone knew he had."

—Greil Marcus, describing the "Comeback Special"

chapter seven

THE COME-BACK

© Ron Galella

In 1964, the Bea-
tles came to the
United States and
forever changed
the American mu-
sic industry. Every-
where they went,
the Fab Four were
greeted by crowds of screaming
teenagers, just as Elvis had been
a few years earlier. They appeared on *The Ed Sullivan Show* on
February 9, 1964, and smashed the ratings record set by Elvis in
1956. Mindful of the Beatles' amazing success, Elvis sent them a
telegram of congratulations on their first Ed Sullivan appearance.

The Beatles—and their compatriots of the 1960s "British
Invasion"—were bringing rock and roll back into the forefront of
the American music scene. Flaunting their long hair and their
mod clothing, the Beatles reinfused rock and roll with the sexuality, rebelliousness, and idealism that had originally defined it. For
the first time since Elvis Presley burst onto the scene in the late
'50s, rock and roll looked and sounded threatening again.

Although they posed a major threat to Presley's career, the
Beatles and other bands that burst onto the scene during the
'60s showed nothing but admiration and respect for the King of
rock and roll. John Lennon stated that "Nothing really affected me
until I heard Elvis. If there hadn't been Elvis, there would not have
been the Beatles." On another occasion, he simply remarked,
"Before Elvis, there was nothing." The Beatles even visited Elvis

during their second North American tour in 1965. On August
27, they stopped by Presley's
Bel Air home and had an im-
promptu jam session that was
supposedly recorded. Unfortunately, tapes from that session
have never surfaced.

While artists such as the Beatles, the Rolling Stones, the
Who, and Bob Dylan were taking America by storm and raising
rock and roll to new heights, Elvis remained in isolation. His last
public performance had taken place on March 25, 1961, when he
played a benefit in Pearl Harbor. From 1955 until his induction
into the Army at the beginning of 1958, Elvis had made over 400
concert appearances across the continent and in Hawaii. After he
was released from the Army, however, he made only two appearances in 1961, and then none at all until 1969, eight years later.

Moreover, Elvis had stopped recording original and exciting
music. Between his triumphant post-Army LP *Elvis is Back* until
his equally successful comeback album in 1969 *From Elvis in
Memphis,* Presley recorded only four nonsoundtrack albums—*His
Hand in Mine, Something for Everybody, Pot Luck,* and *How Great
Thou Art.* Two of these albums, *His Hand in Mine* and *How Great
Thou Art,* were gospel. There were a few other nonsoundtrack
releases during this period; however, these were all hastily put
together collections of previously recorded cuts, such as the four
volumes in the *Golden Records* series. Many of these reissue

Michael Ochs Archive

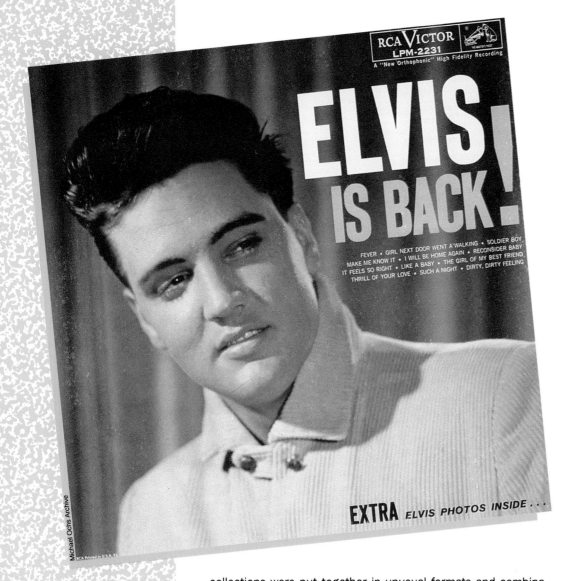

RCA VICTOR
LPM-2231
A "New Orthophonic" High Fidelity Recording

ELVIS
IS BACK!

FEVER • GIRL NEXT DOOR WENT A'WALKING • SOLDIER BOY
MAKE ME KNOW IT • I WILL BE HOME AGAIN • RECONSIDER BABY
IT FEELS SO RIGHT • LIKE A BABY • THE GIRL OF MY BEST FRIEND
THRILL OF YOUR LOVE • SUCH A NIGHT • DIRTY, DIRTY FEELING

EXTRA ELVIS PHOTOS INSIDE . . . .

Michael Ochs Archive

Elvis is Back! was Presley's triumphant post-Army LP and the last quality non-soundtrack rock and roll album he would release for eight years. The album had a 56-week stay on the *Bill-board* bestselling album chart, peaking at number 2 for three weeks.

force in the mainstream music scene. In 1966, Elvis had only one single—"Love Letters"—reach the top twenty of the popular music charts. His biggest selling single in 1967 was "Indescribably Blue," which made a brief appearance on the charts, peaking at number twenty-eight. In the period between 1965 and 1968, Elvis's only truly successful recording was *How Great Thou Art,* a gospel album.

Even his films—once considered a "sure thing" by Hollywood—were becoming less profitable. The most ardent Presley fans would still go to see any movie starring the king; however, the mainstream public had slowly ceased to care. Even Elvis himself began to dread making these movies, sarcastically calling them "travelogues." Elvis was desperate for a change in both his life and his career.

On May 25, 1966, Elvis went to RCA's Nashville recording studio for a three-day session to record a collection of gospel songs, to be released on the album *How Great Thou Art.* This was the first time in two and a half years that Elvis went into the studio to record anything except music for his movies. In addition, it was Elvis's first RCA session ever that was not produced by Chet Atkins. In Atkins's place at the controls was a rising young producer named Felton Jarvis.

Atkins had produced all of Presley's recordings since the singer had signed with RCA in 1956. Many of the early songs that Atkins produced were some of the strongest recordings Presley ever made. Songs such as "Heartbreak Hotel," "Jailhouse Rock," "Paralyzed," and "Don't Be Cruel" were raw, hard-driving, and emotional—perfect examples of Presley's brand of rock and roll. Unfortunately, as Atkins became more involved in the upper reaches of corporate RCA, he became less concerned about what was going on in the studio—particularly with Elvis Presley. Atkins was never really an Elvis Presley fan. He was an established country music guitarist and fan himself, and had worked his way to become head of RCA's Nashville branch, of which Presley was a part. Even at his best, Atkins was a passive producer who never pushed Elvis to his fullest extent. In the early sessions, it was usually Elvis who asked for multiple takes and suggested different arrangements. In a way, although Atkins was behind the controls, these early sessions were produced by Elvis himself. In later years, as the songs became increasingly mediocre and Elvis ceased to care as much about his music, Atkins still never pushed him. He was instead just happy to finish the sessions and get the

collections were put together in unusual formats and combinations. RCA, it seems, took the same attitude as the studios that released Elvis's movies: It didn't matter what material they released or how they released it, as long as they kept up with their regular schedule.

Instead of remaining a vital part of the music industry, Elvis Presley spent his time in Hollywood making three pictures a year—or rather, making the same picture over and over again three times a year. Colonel Parker took Elvis off the touring circuit because it was not nearly as profitable as making movies. Elvis received one million dollars per picture, plus 50 percent of the profits from each, and all his movies made money.

Although Elvis's bank account was healthy, what suffered was his music career. Before 1965, nearly every Elvis Presley album and most of his singles automatically reached the top ten on the music charts. After 1965, however, he ceased to be a driving product out. By 1966, Atkins left producing completely to devote himself full time to his A&R duties. Two years later he was promoted to vice president of RCA.

Unlike Atkins, Felton Jarvis had been an Elvis Presley fan from the beginning. In 1959, he even recorded a novelty record titled "Don't Knock Elvis." Prior to working with Elvis, Jarvis produced records for Fats Domino, Gladys Knight and the Pips, Lloyd Price, and Tommy Roe. *How Great Thou Art* was Jarvis's first assignment as a staff producer for RCA. Four years later, Jarvis would quit RCA to devote himself full time to Elvis's recordings and his live performances. Jarvis remained a loyal member of the Presley camp until the King's death in 1977.

Jarvis was the aggressive producer that Elvis Presley needed to help save his musical career. Jarvis used the same studio and same musicians from the Atkins sessions; however, he combined them with a close attention to detail and an enthusiasm that had been lacking from most of Elvis's 1960s recordings. He also convinced Elvis to demand better material. Because of the poor quality and resulting lack of success of Presley's songs over the previous few years, Elvis was able to loosen Hill and Range's grip on the selection of material he could record. With access to a wider range of music, Jarvis managed to help define a new slick sound for Elvis.

How Great Thou Art (RCA LPM-3758) was released on March 8, 1967. One year later, it was certified a Gold Record by the Record Industry Association of America. The album reached number 18 on the *Billboard* album charts—the highest position for a Presley album in three years—and remained on the charts for 29 weeks. Elvis won his first Grammy Award for the album in the category of Best Sacred Performance. Elvis won just two more Grammy Awards during his career: for Best Inspirational Performance for *He Touched Me* in 1972, and Best Inspirational Performance for the re-release of *How Great Thou Art* in 1974. Ironically, he never won a Grammy Award for any of his rock and roll performances.

The year 1966 marked another big change in Elvis Presley's life. On Christmas Eve of that year, he asked Priscilla Beaulieu to marry him. Priscilla, who actually had been living at Graceland since October, 1962, had been one of the best kept secrets of Elvis Presley's life. After he left Germany for the United States at the beginning of 1960, Elvis had made a point of keeping in touch with Priscilla. Even as he re-embarked on his post-Army movie career and became involved in many well-publicized affairs,

his thoughts remained with Priscilla. He eventually invited her to spend Christmas with him at Graceland in 1960. Because Priscilla was only fifteen years old, it took quite a bit of convincing on Elvis's part to gain permission for her to visit. Finally, after numerous phone calls to her stepfather and repeated assurances that Priscilla would be well chaperoned by Vernon, his new wife, Dee, and Elvis's grandmother Minnie Mae, Captain Beaulieu finally allowed Priscilla to make the journey to the United States to see Elvis.

She returned to Germany on January 2, more in love with Elvis than ever. Elvis, too, had come to realize that Priscilla was the only woman for him. Upon her departure, he immediately called Captain Beaulieu to persuade him to allow Priscilla to finish her schooling in Memphis. After a year and half of receiving persistent phone calls from Elvis and repeated assurances as to his stepdaughter's safety, Captain Beaulieu eventually consented to let Priscilla relocate to Memphis. She moved into Graceland in

During the movie years Elvis ventured into gospel music. Elvis won his first Grammy award for *How Great Thou Art*. He would never win a Grammy for any of his rock and roll albums, only for his gospel performances.

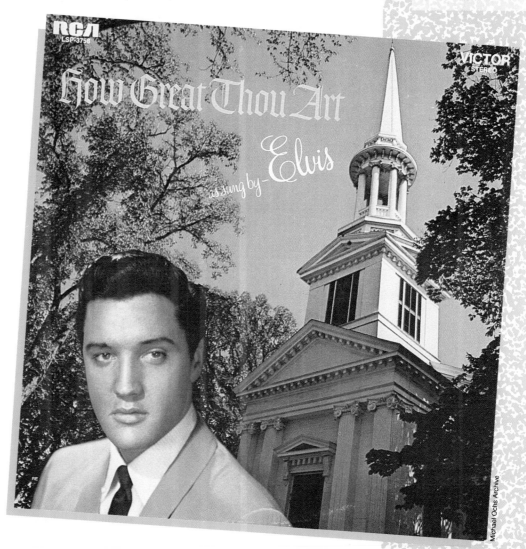

Michael Ochs Archive

Bettmann Archive

Priscilla puts on an album by her favorite singer the day before her wedding in Las Vegas.

stepfather and mother, Major and Mrs. Joseph Beaulieu and Priscilla's brother, Donald; Colonel Tom Parker; Elvis's jeweler, Harry Levitch, and his wife, Frances; Elvis's close friend, George Klein, and his fiancee, Barbara Little; and Elvis's cousin, Patsy Presley Gambill, and her husband, Gee Gee.

Following the ceremony was a small reception and champagne breakfast, at which the newlyweds cut a six-tiered wedding cake, after which they left for their honeymoon in Palm Springs. Upon returning to Graceland, post-honeymoon, Elvis held a second wedding reception for all his friends who were excluded from the actual wedding.

Exactly nine months to the day of Priscilla and Elvis's wedding, on February 1, 1968, at 5:01 p.m., Elvis's only child, Lisa Marie Presley, was born at the Baptist Memorial Hospital in Memphis.

In the meantime, Elvis's musical career continued to rebound. In September, 1967, he headed back into RCA's Nashville studio with Felton Jarvis for an extensive nonsoundtrack recording session. This time, however, he was recording country blues-based rock and roll. Among the songs Elvis recorded during that session were "Big Boss Man," "Guitar Man," "High Heel Sneakers," and "You Don't Know Me." Both "Big Boss Man," written by Al Smith and Luther Dixon, and "Guitar Man," written by Jerry Reed, had been recorded earlier by Reed ("Big Boss Man" in 1961 and "Guitar Man" in 1967). Elvis liked Reed's version of "Guitar Man" so much that he invited him to come into the studio to lay down the lead guitar track.

"High Heel Sneakers" had been written and recorded by Tommy Tucker in 1964 for Checker Records in a session produced by Felton Jarvis. The single reached the eleventh spot on *Billboard*'s Hot 100 Chart. Other artists to record "High Heel Sneakers" were Jerry Lee Lewis (1964), Stevie Wonder (1965), and Jose Feliciano (1968).

The fourth song recorded in the September 1967 session, "You Don't Know Me," was written by Eddie Arnold and Cindy Walker in 1955. The song had been previously recorded by both Arnold and Jerry Vale; however, it had not been particularly successful until Ray Charles made it a hit in 1962. Charles's version sold more than one million copies and soared to number 2 on the Hot 100 chart and number 5 on the Rhythm and Blues chart. Elvis had earlier recorded a version of "You Don't Know Me" for the movie *Clambake*, but was apparently unhappy with the string arrangement of the number and decided to do it again.

October, 1962, at the age of seventeen. Once settled in Memphis, Priscilla attended the Immaculate Conception High School. After she graduated on June 14, 1963, Elvis enrolled Priscilla in the Patricia Stevens Finishing School.

For four years, Colonel Parker's remarkable publicity machine was able to keep Priscilla's relationship with Elvis out of the press. Parker officially described Priscilla as a child whose parents were living overseas and wanted her to finish her schooling in the United States. By letting her live at Graceland, Elvis was simply doing a favor for an old Army buddy. By the end of 1966, however, the Colonel was not sure for how much longer he could keep Priscilla a secret. So Elvis's 1966 marriage proposal was prompted not solely by his own desires, but also, at least partially, by the Colonel's prodding.

Five months later, on May 1, 1967, Elvis and Priscilla were married in a small, secret ceremony held in a private suite at the Las Vegas Aladdin Hotel. The wedding ceremony, which lasted only ten minutes, was presided over by Nevada Supreme Court Justice David Zenoff. Priscilla's thirteen-year-old sister, Michelle, served as the maid of honor and Joe Esposito and Marty Lacker as the best men. Guests at the Beaulieu-Presley wedding included: Elvis's father, Vernon Presley, and his wife, Dee; Priscilla's

Motion Picture & TV Archives

Elvis and Priscilla were wed on May 1, 1967 at the Aladdin Hotel in Las Vegas. Here, they pose for the cameras while cutting the wedding cake.

Wide World Photos

Although the ceremony was small and private, the two newlyweds did face the public after their vows were taken. Elvis, 32, and Priscilla, 21, hold hands and kiss for the camera.

While the commercial success of these recordings was only moderate at best—"Big Boss Man"/"You Don't Know Me" (RCA 47-9341) reached number 38 during its six-week stint on the charts and "Guitar Man"/"High Heel Sneakers" (RCA 47-9426) peaked at number 43 and again lasted six weeks—this session did mark a return to artistic respectability for Presley. Elvis was back to recording the type of music that had made him great— blues-based, beat-oriented rock and roll. The songs were recorded with a degree of professionalism and attention to detail that had been lacking in his earlier 1960s recordings. Elvis, along with the guidance of Felton Jarvis, was beginning to develop a slicker, more polished sound that carried over better in contemporary music of the 1960s.

Still, Elvis wanted more from his career. He yearned to regain the popularity and respectability that he had lost during his movie years. He needed a vehicle that would catapult him back into the public eye to help him reestablish his position in popular music. In January, 1968, Colonel Parker and NBC announced plans for an hour-long Christmas special to be aired the following December. This would be Elvis's first television appearance since the 1960 Frank Sinatra special and the first time he performed in front of a live audience in nearly seven years.

Colonel Parker envisioned the special as a standard Christmas show in the style of a Perry Como or Andy Williams offering. Elvis would greet the audience, sing a few traditional Christmas carols, perhaps appear in a skit or two, and then sign off, wishing the nation happy holidays. The show's producer/director Steve Binder, however, had a different idea.

Like Felton Jarvis, Steve Binder had been an ardent Elvis Presley fan since the 1950s. The Elvis he loved, however, was not the homogenized, nonthreatening, celluloid Elvis of the big screen, but the young, rebellious, sexy Elvis that had incensed church groups and caused parents many sleepless nights. Binder remembered the energy of Elvis's music and the thrill and excitement that his live performances could evoke. Binder also sensed that Elvis still carried that vitality and that it could be captured in the television special.

By this time, Presley's career was on the rocks. Considered a has-been by many, he was fighting for his rightful place in history. Binder believed that if Elvis appeared in a television special like the one Colonel Parker envisioned that it could be the final nail in the coffin that was built by ten years of bad movies and even worse soundtrack albums. He was determined not to let that happen. Colonel Parker, however, was equally determined to have the special done his way. After weeks of heated telephone calls and arguments with the Colonel, Binder eventually went to Elvis himself to plead his case.

Elvis felt extremely nervous about putting himself on the line by performing live again, but he also realized that Steve Binder was probably right. This television special would be his last chance to prove that he was still a mover and a shaker and not just a curiosity that had flared briefly on the music scene during the 1950s. So, for the first time in his career, Elvis proceeded against the Colonel's wishes. He would take a risk and do the special Binder's way.

Both Felton Jarvis and Steve Binder proved invaluable to Presley's career. In his own fashion, each man pushed Elvis to the limits of his talents. By refusing to be simple "yes men," the record producer and the television director helped Elvis to restart his stuttering career. Not since Sam Phillips had there been

anyone in Elvis's camp that pushed him to strive for growth and quality in his work. Colonel Parker certainly did not fill that role. Parker had no artistic integrity whatsoever; he was a manager who helped Elvis—and himself—make a lot of money. That was the extent of his contribution—everything the colonel did, he did for the quick buck.

The Christmas special, now fully under Binder's control, consisted of several elaborate production numbers, as well as what became known as the "pit" segment. The pit segment itself was actually broken down into two sections: one in which Elvis stood

Exactly nine months to the day after they were wed (February 1, 1968) Priscilla gave birth to Lisa Marie.

Wide World Photos

Colonel Tom Parker wanted Elvis's 1968 special to be a traditional Christmas in the style of Andy Williams. For the first time in his life, Elvis rebelled against his manager. To emphasize the point, he dressed completely in black leather for most of the show.

Personally Photos, Inc.

by himself on a small stage in the round, surrounded by fewer than 100 people in a studio audience, and another in which he sat on the same stage for an informal jam session with members of his old band, Scotty Moore and D.J. Fontana (Bill Black had died of a brain tumor three years earlier), as well as musicians Charlie Hodge and Alan Fortas.

Rehearsals for the pit segment took place in Burbank on June 17, 18, and 19, 1968, and the prerecorded musical tracks for the production numbers were laid down on June 21 and 22 at Western Recorders in Los Angeles. (Elvis had recently completed recording the soundtrack of *Live a Little, Love a Little* [1968] at Western.)

On June 27, at 6:00 p.m., formal taping of the show began in tiny Studio 4 on NBC's Burbank lot, marking Elvis Presley's first appearance in front of a live audience in nearly eight years. A second show was taped at 8:00 p.m. and then two more on June 29 at 6:00 p.m. and 8:00 p.m. Just before the taping of each show, Colonel Parker busied himself rearranging the audience and placing pretty girls in the front near Elvis.

Elvis was clearly nervous as he began his first song. He knew that to many members of his audience, his career had become something of a joke over the past few years. He was unsure as to whether he would be able to generate that old excitement in front of a large audience, yet as the first few chords rang out, his self-confidence returned and he regained his legendary magic touch. Elvis was in perfect form. With his slicked-back hair and long sideburns, and attired in a tight, black leather suit, he cut a sleek, handsome figure. He was suntanned and thinner than he had been in years. Most importantly, his voice was stronger than ever. It was a wiser, more mature, and more cynical Elvis who ripped through a set of old rock and roll classics and powerful ballads. The intimate setting of the pit segment was the perfect venue for Elvis to acquaint himself with a new generation of fans.

Elvis performed the first few songs alone on the stage, either playing guitar and singing or just standing alone with a mike, belting out the tunes to the audience sitting right at his feet. The band, complete with a full orchestra, played offstage behind the audience. There was nothing to divert the audience's eyes from the star's mesmerizing performance.

In the later part of the pit segment, Elvis sat on a chair placed in a circle among the members of his old band, each playing an acoustic guitar while D.J. Fontana pounded out the beat on the back of a guitar case. At this point in the show, a completely relaxed Elvis bantered with his band members and the audience in between loose, yet powerful renditions of his old hits and standard rhythm and blues numbers. According to the script, Elvis was supposed to reminisce about the old days and talk about his music. Instead, he just jammed with his old friends and had a good time. Despite the scripted instructions, Elvis refused to open up and talk about himself. Nevertheless, he did joke around with the band and the fans. Indeed, at one point during the segment, he stopped the band in the middle of a song as his lip curled in a classic Elvis snarl. He pointed up to his snarl and said, "Wait a minute...wait a minute. My lip's stuck." As the band laughed he continued, "I've got news for you. I did twenty-nine pictures like that."

The final taping of the production numbers took place on June 30. The special aired on NBC at 9:00 p.m. on December 3, 1968. As the show opened, a blue neon light spelled out "Elvis" in glowing letters across a black screen. Without a word spoken, the band kicked into the first chords of a song and the show cut to an extreme close-up of Elvis's face as he sang the first lines of "Trouble:" "Are you looking for trouble? / Well, you've come to the right place."

From "Trouble," the band immediately struck up the first chords of "Guitar Man," as the camera pulled back to show Elvis standing in front of a gigantic twenty-foot (6m) red neon logo with dozens of dancers all dressed like Elvis holding guitars. It was an incredibly self-indulgent opening, yet it served its purpose in portraying the myth of Elvis Presley as a star larger than life.

Despite the invaluable input of Steve Binder, the weakest segments of the whole show were the large-scale production numbers, the segments over which he had most control. Perhaps the best production number, a bordello setting in which Elvis sings "Let Yourself Go," was cut from the special because censors thought it too racy.

In a last-ditch effort to regain some control, Colonel Parker demanded that Elvis close the show with a Christmas song. Binder, however, held his ground and persuaded Elvis to sing a song written by the show's musical director, Earl Brown. The choice was a wise one. "If I Can Dream" is an above average, if a bit naive, song that Elvis transformed, through the emotional strength of his performance, into a testament to his career and his beliefs.

Elvis opened the special with a medley of "Trouble" and "Guitar Man" performed in front of a giant neon-lit sign reading, simply, "ELVIS".

Personality Photos, Inc.

The instrumental tracks for "If I Can Dream" were recorded first, on June 21, 1968, at Western Recorders, and Elvis's vocal track was recorded live during the taping of the segment at NBC on June 29. RCA released the song as a single in late October in anticipation of the special. It hit *Billboard*'s Hot 100 chart in November, but did not make its big surge until after the show aired. By January 1969, "If I Can Dream"/"Edge of Reality" (RCA 47-9670) had reached number 12 on the charts, where it remained for 13 weeks. It was Elvis's biggest hit since "I'm Yours" (a song recorded in 1961) made it to number 11 in 1965. The soundtrack album, *Elvis—TV Special* (RCA LPM-4088), rose to the eighth spot and stayed on the album charts for thirty-two weeks. The album was certified a Gold Record on August 27, 1969.

Although the 1968 NBC Christmas special is officially titled "Elvis," it almost immediately became known simply as "The Comeback Special." Truly, Elvis had staged a remarkable, triumphant comeback. The show catapulted him back into the forefront of the music scene. Critics were quick to recognize Elvis Presley's accomplishments. Rock critic Greil Marcus enthused, "If there was ever music that bleeds, this was it...he gave everything that he had—more than anyone knew he had." John Landau wrote, "There is something magical about watching a man who has lost himself find his way back home. He sang with the kind of power people no longer expect from rock and roll singers." And *Record World* declared, "It wasn't the old Elvis, trading on the nostalgia of early rock and obsolete Ed Sullivan censorship. It was a moddish performer, virile and humorous and vibrating the nervousness of the times."

Elvis Presley himself was not ready to simply rest on the laurels of his television triumph. He intended his comeback to be more than just a one-night stand—rather, it would be just the beginning of his resurgence as an important player in the rock-and-roll game. Almost immediately after the special aired, he returned to the studio to record more music. In mid-January 1969, he went in for a ten-day session at American Sound Studios in Memphis. This was Elvis's first recording session in Memphis since his Sun Records days.

Located at 827 Danny Thomas Street, American Sound Studios was founded by Chips Moman and Bob Crewe. What attracted Elvis to the studio was its house band, which was considered one of the best in the country. Led by Tommy Cogbill on bass, the band included guitarist Reggie Young; organist Bobby

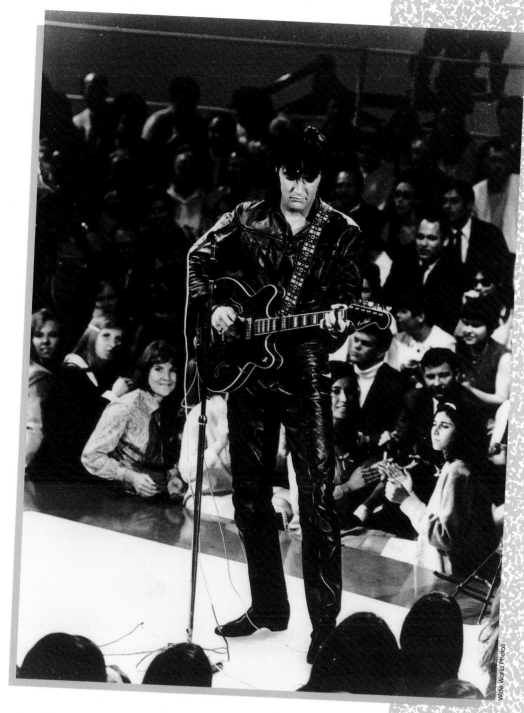

Wide World Photos

Emmons, who had played with Bill Black's band after Black left Elvis; former Jerry Lee Lewis drummer Gene Christman; bassist Mike Leech; and guitarists Ed Kollis and John Hughey. American was one of the most successful new studios in the country, having produced 125 chart records in four years. At the time Elvis began recording there, the studio's biggest stars were The Box Tops, fronted by the young Alex Chilton, and Dusty Springfield. When Elvis walked into American Studios he looked around and said, "What a funky, funky place."

Attired in black leather, a slim Elvis recaptured some of his earlier magic.

The original ten-day recording session had to be cut short because Elvis came down with laryngitis; however, he did return in February to complete five more days of recording. In what was perhaps his most productive and satisfying recording session ever, Elvis completed thirty-five songs in a total of eleven days over the two sessions. Among these recordings were three singles that would crack the top ten—"In the Ghetto," "Suspicious Minds," and "Don't Cry, Daddy," as well as enough solid album tracks to fill two albums.

Of all the singles to come out of the American Studios recording sessions, the most successful was "Suspicious Minds." The song was written and originally recorded by Mark James at American Studios; however, his release never charted. Elvis's version of the song was actually a splice of three different takes. Horns were added at United Recording Studios in Las Vegas. "Suspicious Minds"/"You'll Think of Me" (RCA 47-9764) was

released in September, 1969, and immediately began to shoot up *Billboard*'s Hot 100 chart. By November it had climbed all the way to the top, replacing the Temptations' number 1 hit "I Can't Get Next to You." After one week in the top spot, however, it was replaced by "Wedding Bell Blues" by The Fifth Dimension. Despite being bumped from first place, "Suspicious Minds" remained near the top of the charts for fifteen weeks. It was to be Elvis's last chart-topping hit.

"In the Ghetto" was written by Mac Davis and was originally offered to the Righteous Brothers and Sammy Davis Jr., both of whom turned it down. RCA released Elvis's recording, "In the Ghetto"/"Any Day Now" (RCA 47-9741), on April 15, 1969. The single reached number 3 during its thirteen-week stay on the Hot 100 chart. Despite its success on the popular chart and overseas (it was a number-2 hit in Great Britain), the song peaked at a disappointing number 60 on the country chart. Dolly Parton covered the song later in 1969 and her version went to number 50 on the country chart.

"Don't Cry, Daddy" was another Mac Davis song. It was the third top-ten record from this single recording session. Released in November, 1969, the song featured Ronnie Milsap singing background and Ed Kollis on harmonica. "Don't Cry, Daddy"/"Rubberneckin'" (RCA 47-9768) peaked at number 6 on the *Billboard* Hot 100 chart. The number 1 song at the time was "Suspicious Minds."

Other notable songs from the two American Studios Sessions include: "Kentucky Rain," "Long Black Limousine," "Wearing That Loved On Look," "I'm Moving On," "Only the Strong Survive," "Stranger in My Own Home Town," and "It Keeps Right on a Hurtin'." The thirty-five songs completed were used in two albums: the seminal *From Elvis in Memphis* (RCA LSP-4155) and double live/studio album *From Memphis to Vegas/From Vegas to Memphis* (RCA LSP-6020).

Suddenly, Elvis Presley was a top-ten hit maker again. In a little over a year, Elvis had produced four top-ten singles and six gold records. His television special was a resounding success with fans and critics alike and had introduced him to a whole new generation of fans. In addition, the special made Elvis realize how much he missed performing. He had proven that he still had the magic on television and in the studio, now he needed to prove that he could generate the same excitement live. It was time to go back on the road.

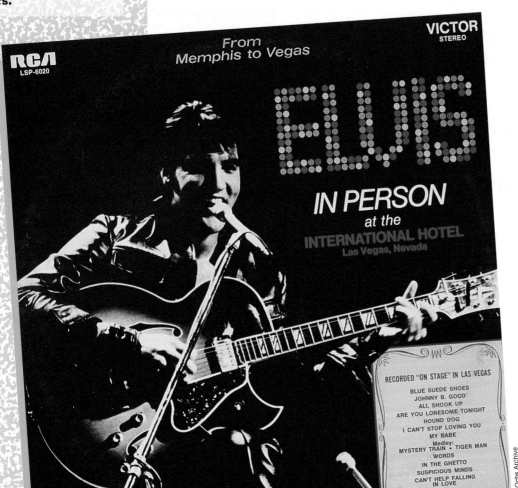

RCA
LSP-6020

VICTOR
STEREO

From
Memphis to Vegas

ELVIS

IN PERSON
at the
INTERNATIONAL HOTEL
Las Vegas, Nevada

RECORDED "ON STAGE" IN LAS VEGAS
BLUE SUEDE SHOES
JOHNNY B. GOOD
ALL SHOOK UP
ARE YOU LONESOME TONIGHT
HOUND DOG
I CAN'T STOP LOVING YOU
MY BABE
Medley:
MYSTERY TRAIN · TIGER MAN
WORDS
IN THE GHETTO
SUSPICIOUS MINDS
CAN'T HELP FALLING
IN LOVE

Michael Ochs Archive

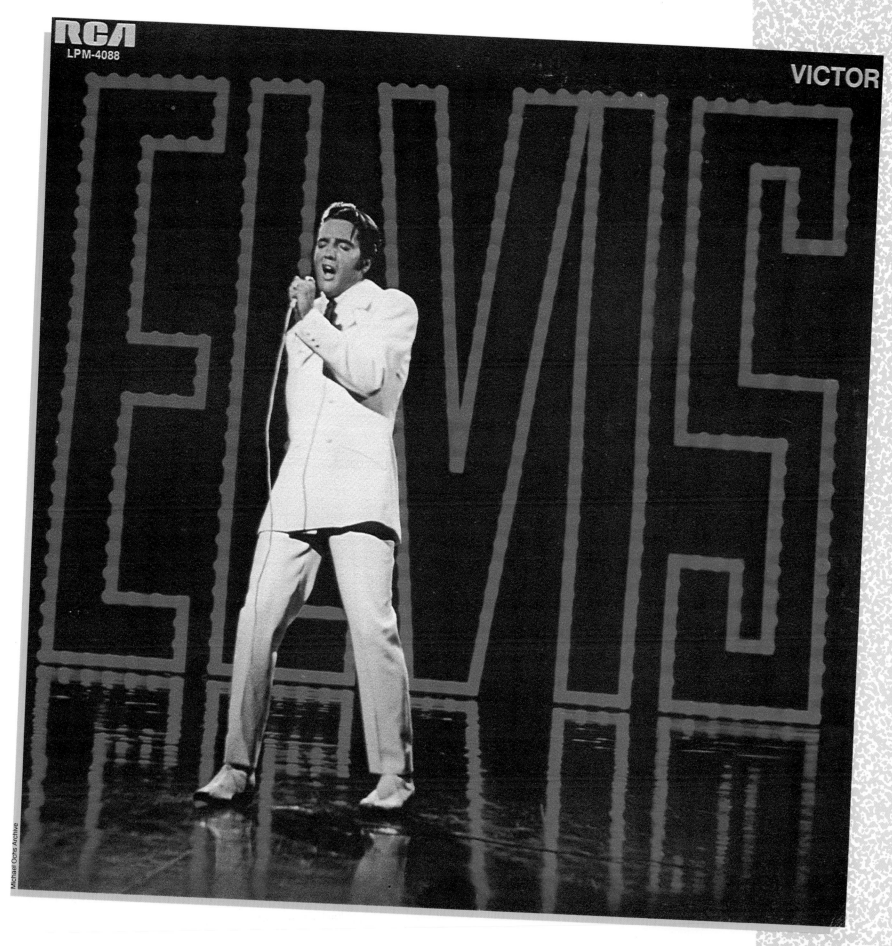

RCA
LPM-4088

VICTOR

ELVIS

Michael Ochs Archive

Motion Picture & TV Archives

"There have been contenders, but there is only one King."
—Bruce Springsteen

chapter eight

THE FINAL YEARS

Elvis started the 1970s with a renewed enthusiasm. He was again at the top of the music world, but excessive touring, poor health, and drug use would prove his undoing before the decade ended.

Three Elvis Presley movies were released in 1969, the year he made his musical comeback—*Charro!*, *The Trouble With Girls*, and *A Change of Habit*. By this point, however, not many people cared about his movies; he was back to making music again, and that's what was important. As a result, although none of them actually lost money, all three films were box office disappointments.

Throughout the 1960s, Colonel Parker had not booked Elvis into any live shows because they were more work and were not nearly as profitable as making three pictures a year. Elvis made an average of $1 million per movie plus a large percentage of the profits. By 1969, however, audiences were dwindling and studios were becoming reluctant to pay Elvis's $1 million base fee, let alone split the film's meager profits. In addition, Elvis had long ago grown tired of making movies. Finally, he told the Colonel not to commit him to anything except a high-quality project.

After Elvis's triumphant television comeback and his string of top-ten singles, the Colonel began to think that it was time for the King to return to the stage. Elvis was anxious to perform and audiences were hungry to see him live for the first time in eight years. Colonel Parker also realized that putting Elvis on tour could be extremely profitable. The original plan was to book Elvis into a series of stadium gigs, starting off with a show in the Houston Astrodome. Elvis was to receive $100,000 per show. Colonel Parker figured that even if Elvis did just two concerts a week for five weeks, he would be able to make the same amount of money that he would have earned from making one film, which required three months of filming.

As Parker began looking into stadium dates for Elvis, he was contacted by the 1,500-room International Hotel in Las Vegas about booking Elvis for two weeks of shows in their brand new Showroom Internationale, the biggest show room in Vegas. The International was willing to pay Elvis 1 million dollars for the two weeks, at two shows per night. This deal looked perfect to Parker. Elvis would make his cool million while performing in what Parker considered the biggest show-business town in the country. In addition, Parker, an avid gambler, would have unlimited access to the casinos, while receiving red-carpet treatment.

Elvis was a bit wary about returning to the stage in Las Vegas. It had been thirteen years since the only time he ever played Vegas in a series of shows that were best described as disastrous. Elvis was uncomfortable about making his concert return in the same town that had snubbed him so badly in 1956. Yet even he realized that the terms of the deal were so inviting that he could not pass it up.

In early July, Elvis went to Las Vegas to hire a band and begin rehearsals. Elvis put together a band of crack musicians led by James Burton on guitar. Burton had been a staple of the rock and roll music scene since 1957, when he recorded and toured with Ricky Nelson. (In the late 1980s and early 1990s, Burton went on to play with Presley namesake Elvis Costello). Other members of the band included drummer Ronnie Tutt, bassist Jerry Scheff, keyboard player Larry Muhoberac, guitarists John Wilkinson and Charlie Hodge, and the gospel vocal group the Sweet Inspirations.

All shows for the two-week stint sold out almost as soon as tickets went on sale. Two more weeks were added to the run and tickets for those shows were gone in a matter of days.

On July 31, 1969, Elvis made his return to the stage after an eight-year hiatus. On a darkened stage, the band rang out the first few chords of "Baby, I Don't Care" as Elvis confidently walked on, lit by a sole spotlight. As he grabbed the mike and began to sing, the lights went up and the music was nearly drowned out by the deafening roar of the crowd. Elvis and the band pounded through the hour-long set as if they had been playing together for years. Between songs Elvis would joke with the crowd, at one point offering an explanation as to why he returned to the stage: "I got tired of singing to the guys I beat up in the motion pictures." The show was tight and slick, yet spontaneous and electrifying, and Elvis was able to sustain the excitement for the entire fifty-seven shows he performed over the next four weeks. In short, it was the most successful show Las Vegas had ever seen. For four weeks, the town belonged to Elvis, and when he completed his last show on August 28, America was still clamoring for more.

It was in this Vegas show that Elvis developed some of the conventions that were to mark Elvis Presley concerts throughout the '70s. He would bend down at the edge of the stage and kiss or hold hands with women in the audience, or take a hankie from one of them, wipe his brow, and hand it back. Although he was not yet wearing his trademark jumpsuits, he did have on a modified black karate suit and he would perform karate moves during musical breaks in some of his songs. (Ever since the Army, Elvis had been an avid practitioner of karate. He eventually achieved the level of seventh-degree black belt under karate master Kang Rhee.) Elvis closed this first show with "What'd I Say," but then came on for an encore of "Can't Help Falling in Love," the song he used to end the rest of his concerts over the next eight years.

Critics praised Elvis's long awaited return to the stage:

"Elvis was supernatural, his own resurrection."—*Rolling Stone*

"[Presley was] immediately affable...very much in command of the entire scene."—*Variety*

"Elvis Presley electrifies Vegas in his triumphant return to the stage."—*Billboard*

"There are several unbelievable things about Elvis, but the most incredible is his staying power in a world where meteoric careers fade like shooting stars."—*Newsweek*

Elvis takes Vegas by storm at the International Hotel in 1969. He did fifty-seven shows there between July 31 and August 28 of that year.

Personality Photos, Inc.

Immediately following this second Las Vegas run, Elvis took the show on the road, beginning with three nights and six shows (all of them sell-outs) at the Houston Astrodome. Tickets for the Astrodome shows were only one dollar, so that even Elvis's poorest fans could afford to see him. Elvis received $100,000 a show for the six shows, plus a percentage of the gate, earning him more than $1.2 million for three days.

Over the next seven years, Elvis Presley was on the road constantly, doing thousands of shows in hundreds of cities, and returning each year for a long stint in Las Vegas. Fans continued to flock to his shows, and nearly every one of them sold out, but the incessant touring schedule began to take its toll on Elvis's personal life. He became increasingly dependent on a wide variety of prescription drugs and fought a constant battle against weight gain. The touring also took a toll on his marriage. For the most part, Elvis did not like to take Priscilla on tour with him, preferring her to remain at home in Graceland or Los Angeles. At the same time, Priscilla was feeling the need to assert herself and making an attempt to become her own person. She had spent more than half of her teenage years with Elvis, living at Graceland and trying to be the woman that Elvis wanted her to be. Her interests, her hobbies, even her appearance was closely controlled by Elvis Presley and after four years of marriage, she was beginning to realize that maybe there was more to life than just being Elvis Presley's wife. Elvis sensed her dissatisfaction, and suggested a hobby. He introduced her to martial-arts instructor Mike Stone, from whom she could learn karate.

Elvis first saw Mike Stone at the Karate Tournament of Champions in Honolulu, where Stone lived with his wife, Fran. Elvis later met him in 1971 in Las Vegas, where Stone was working as a bodyguard for record producer Phil Spector. Soon after that meeting, Priscilla began taking karate lessons from Stone. The two became very close friends and eventually, lovers.

By February 23, 1972, Priscilla's life as Mrs. Elvis Presley had become intolerable, so she took Lisa Marie and moved out of Graceland to Los Angeles. There, she continued her relationship with Mike Stone. It was Red West who broke the news to Elvis that Priscilla was seeing Stone. According to West, in 1973, during a drug-induced stupor, Elvis became so enraged by the affair that he ordered Red's cousin Sonny West to hire a hit man to kill Stone. Whether or not Elvis actually ordered the killing is a matter of debate; however, nothing ever came of it. On another night,

Above: The outside of the then-new International Hotel. Elvis smashed all existing Las Vegas attendance records while performing there. Opposite page: Early on in the 1970s, Elvis began performing in the flashy jumpsuits that soon became his trademark style.

By the end of the run, Elvis had broken all Las Vegas attendance records. In one month he played for 57 different sold-out houses, for a total of 101,500.

Elvis was back at the International Hotel in January, 1970, just six months after his first triumphant engagement there. Many people thought it was a mistake for him to return to perform in Vegas so soon, particularly in what is traditionally a slow season for Las Vegas. However, when tickets went on sale, the scheduled twenty-nine shows sold out immediately. Just as in his first engagement, twenty-nine more shows were added just to keep up with ticket demand.

according to Elvis biographer Jerry Hopkins, Elvis poured his heart out to friend Ed Parker: "She has everything money can buy, Ed—cars, homes, an expense account. And she knows that all she has to do is ask, and I'll get her whatever she wants. I can't understand, Ed. I love that woman."

On January 8, 1973, his thirty-eighth birthday, Elvis filed for divorce in California citing that "irreconcilable differences" had caused the breakdown of the marriage. The divorce was finalized on October 11, 1973, in Santa Monica with Priscilla gaining full custody of the couple's five-year-old daughter, Lisa Marie. Priscilla received a financial settlement of about $2 million, half to be paid at the time of the divorce and the other half to be paid over the next ten years. Elvis was also ordered to pay $4,000 a month in child support.

Throughout the beginning of the 1970s, Elvis's career continued to flourish. He made two more films—*Elvis: That's the Way It Is* (1970) and *Elvis On Tour*—both were concert films. After *A Change of Habit* (1969), Elvis Presley never made another dramatic film. Of the two concert films, *Elvis: That's the Way It Is* is the best. Directed by renowned documentary filmmaker Denis Sanders (Sanders won an Academy Award for his landmark documentary *Czechoslovakia 1968*), the film centers around the rehearsals and performances of Elvis's second International Hotel engagement. The film was edited from the first five shows of the Vegas run interspersed with candid scenes and interviews. Five cameras and a forty-person crew were used to capture the excitement of a Presley concert. While the live performance sequences are truly electrifying, the most interesting moments of the film are the backstage glimpses. For the first time, the public was able to see the real Elvis Presley. These behind-the-scenes images show an Elvis Presley who laughs, gets angry and frustrated, and at times, feels a little scared. The movie also reveals an Elvis Presley who is at once never alone, yet is also extremely isolated—a man, who for the vast majority of his adult life, could not go out in public.

The event that is perhaps Elvis Presley's last great triumph took place in January, 1973, just a few days after he filed for divorce from Priscilla. On January 9, 1973, Elvis flew to Hawaii to begin rehearsals for *Elvis: Aloha From Hawaii,* a worldwide live television broadcast of a benefit concert for the Kuiokolani Lee Cancer Fund. (Kuiokolani Lee was a legendary figure in Hawaiian music who died of cancer.)

Paul Caruso Collection

For several months before the concert, Elvis had begun an intense fitness program in order to trim down for the show. After seeing Elvis's transformation, Sonny West commented that Elvis was "thin as a rake and handsomer than ten movie stars."

Elvis rehearsed for two days, and then on January 12 he held a dress rehearsal in front of 6,000 fans at Honolulu International Center Arena. This dress rehearsal was later heard on many bootleg albums, as well as the 1988 RCA album *The Alternate Aloha* (RCA 6985-1-R).

The actual concert took place on January 14 at 12:30 a.m., Honolulu time, and was beamed via the Intelsat IV communications satellite to Japan, South Korea, Australia, New Zealand, South Vietnam, Thailand, the Philippines (where ratings hit a remarkable 92 percent), and even parts of Communist China. The next day it was broadcast to twenty-eight nations in Europe. The North American edition of the concert was broadcast on April 4, 1973 at 8:30 p.m. on NBC. Five songs were added to that broadcast.

All in all, approximately one billion people in more than forty countries watched *Elvis: Aloha From Hawaii,* making it the most-watched television event in history.

After the Aloha concert, things swiftly began to go downhill for Elvis Presley. Elvis's decline into prescription drug dependency continued unabated, and despite his constant touring, he became more isolated than ever. He almost never ventured out into the daylight, instead rising at about 4:00 in the afternoon and staying up all night. When he was on tour, Elvis ordered the windows of his hotel rooms lined with aluminum foil to block out all sunlight.

Elvis's weight problem also worsened. Ever since the 1960s, Elvis had fought a never-ending war with his weight. He was a binge eater who could devour a pound (2.5 kg) of bacon and a dozen eggs at a sitting and follow that with a quart (about 1 l) or two of ice cream. Then, knowing he had a public engagement coming up, Elvis would go on a crash diet to lose his extra girth. As a younger man, Elvis was able to gain thirty-five or forty pounds (88–100 kg) and then lose it in a matter of weeks through starvation dieting. During the 1970s, however, dropping the added weight became more and more difficult. Much of the medication that Elvis relied on was intended to help him trim down. He took injections to curb his appetite and help him lose weight, as well as to return to him some of the energy he lacked as a result of eating less. To counter the amphetamine effects of the diet drugs, Elvis also took sleeping pills to help him relax.

The combination of his fluctuating weight and his reliance on various addictive drugs led to a dramatic decline in Elvis's health during these years. He developed an enlarged colon, which led to serious digestive problems and caused him constant pain. This intestinal condition was largely caused by the uncontrolled and unceasing loss and gain of weight, plus his unhealthy dieting strategies, which swung from virtual self-starvation to an excessive use of laxatives, causing his colon to lose its ability to contract. To ease the pain of his colon difficulties, Elvis added more and more painkillers into his drug-taking routine.

As the 1970s continued, Elvis's health deteriorated. He was hospitalized several times for a variety of health problems, including intestinal blockage, enlarged colon, glaucoma, eye strain, pneumonia, exhaustion, and gastric flu. He was admitted to the Baptist Hospital in Memphis, where he stayed in a suite of rooms in which, as was his habit, the windows had been lined with

Elvis belts out a song during the taping of *Elvis: Aloha from Hawaii*. This live televised concert turned out to be the most-watched television event in history at that time.

Personality Photos, Inc.

Motion Picture & TV Archives

Elvis continued his grueling tour schedule throughout the mid-1970s despite his constant battles with exhaustion, obesity, and poor health. Here he sings at the Nassau Coliseum, Long Island, New York, on July 19, 1975.

© Ron Galella

Alabama as a young child. He later earned a Ph.D. from the University of Tennessee and an M.D. from Vanderbilt University. He moved to Memphis to set up a practice, where he met Elvis in 1966. Elvis had been suffering from a bad cold. George Klein, Elvis's friend since Humes High, recommended that he be treated by Dr. Nick. Klein's wife, Barbara, worked in Dr. Nick's office. Over the years, Dr. Nick encouraged Elvis to take up a healthier lifestyle. It was Nichopoulos who cultivated Elvis's interest in racquetball. Conversely, however, Dr. Nick prescribed dizzying amounts of a variety of pharmaceuticals for Elvis. He maintained that these drugs were simply to help Elvis with his physical and emotional problems. However, when looking at the laundry list of drugs on the last prescription Dr. Nick wrote for Elvis, one can't help but wonder about the doctor's medical ethics:

> Dilaudid—50–4 mg tablets
> Quaalude—150–300 mg tablets
> Dexedrine—100–5 mg tablets
> Percodan—100 tablets
> Amytal—100–3 gram capsules
> 12 half gram ampules
> Biphetamine—100–20 mg spansules

All of these drugs were issued on one prescription written for Elvis the day before he died. Between January 20 and August 16, 1977, Dr. Nick prescribed 5,684 doses of strong narcotics and amphetamines for Elvis—an average of 25 doses a day. In addition, Dr. Nick allegedly wrote prescriptions out to members of Elvis's entourage, knowing full well that the drugs were actually for Elvis himself.

Dr. Nick was richly rewarded for his services. Elvis once gave him a $40,000 yellow Cadillac and loaned him monies totalling more than $300,000. These loans were made interest-free and the notes were payable sometime in the next century. This exchange of money raised many questions regarding the doctor/patient relationship at work, as well as Dr. Nick's medical standards. In September, 1979, the Tennessee Board of Medical Examiners charged Dr. Nick with "indiscriminately prescribing 5,300 pills and vials for Elvis Presley in the seven months before his death." The following January, he was barred from practicing medicine while the Tennessee Medical Board completed an investigation of his practices and he was eventually indicted by a Shelby County Grand jury for illegally prescribing drugs. He was later acquitted of the charges.

aluminum foil. Linda Thompson, his girlfriend for four years during the 1970s, usually stayed in the hospital with him. Elvis's final visit to the hospital lasted from April 1 to April 6, 1977, just four months before his death.

Elvis Presley's personal physician was Dr. George Nichopoulos, or "Dr. Nick," as he was known in the Elvis camp. Born in Ridgeway, Pennsylvania, in 1927, George Nichopoulos moved to

By 1977, Elvis Presley had given up his attempts to lose weight. He began the year, as he did every year of the 1970s, with a major tour beginning February 12 in Hollywood, Florida, and ending four months later at the Market Square Arena in Indianapolis. (The Market Square Arena date would prove to be Elvis's last concert.) In between, he played fifty-five shows in forty-seven different cities all over the United States. His health was extremely poor and he worked in constant pain. In fact, he was briefly hospitalized for exhaustion in the middle of the tour.

A CBS-TV special entitled *Elvis in Concert* was filmed at the Omaha Civic Auditorium on June 19, 1977, and at the Rushmore Civic Center in Rapid City, South Dakota, on June 21. After his death, the special was quickly completed and aired on October 3, 1977. It shows a grossly overweight Elvis Presley struggling through his songs. When he speaks, his words are slurred, and he moves around the stage like a man aged sixty-two instead of forty-two. He tries desperately to live up to the myth he created for himself, but the fire and the passion are gone. His voice, for the most part, lacks the range and strength that made him the most dynamic performer of his time, yet on a few songs he manages to garner enough intensity to belt out an emotional rendition and bring memories of past glories rushing back. Then he falters again, a sad caricature of a once-great singer.

On June 26, Elvis went back to Memphis to rest for two months before beginning another tour on August 17 in Portland, Maine. Elvis dreaded going back on tour, telling a member of his entourage, "I'm so tired of being Elvis Presley." Yet, Colonel Parker kept the dates booked—the money had to keep coming in.

Elvis was also deeply disturbed by a book that had been written by his former bodyguards and longtime Memphis Mafia members Red West, Sonny West, and Dave Hebler, with the aid of *National Star* writer Steve Dunleavy. *Elvis, What Happened?* is a no-holds-barred exposé of Elvis's drug use, temper tantrums, and emotional state. It is a trashily written tell-all that according to the authors was intended to force Elvis to wake up and face his problems. The book, however, reads more like an embittered attack on Elvis and a way to exploit his fame to make a lot of money. Elvis had asked Vernon to fire the three bodyguards on July 13, 1976. The official reason was that Elvis needed to cut expenses. It is more likely, however, that Elvis had them fired because he was under a lot of pressure from a series of lawsuits brought by fans who were roughed up by the bodyguards.

When the book was published, Elvis felt betrayed. He could not believe that friends he had loved and trusted would publish such a book about him. (In hindsight, this is very ironic, considering that just about everybody who had any day-to-day contact with Elvis wrote a book about him after his death. Very few, however, were as vicious as *Elvis, What Happened?*) Equally worrisome were the possible repercussions to his career—would Elvis's fans cease to love him when they found out about his problems?

Elvis, What Happened? was published in July, 1977 and immediately aroused a wave of controversy. Instead of rejecting him, as he had feared, many of Elvis's ardent fans seemed to rise to his defense. Many simply insisted that the book was filled with vicious lies. Others reacted with anger at the bodyguards for their disloyalty to Elvis. Bookstores across the South reported that copies of the book were being vandalized by Presley fans in order to make them unsellable.

Despite the show of support, however, Elvis was convinced that his career was doomed.

Just after midnight on August 16, the day before Elvis was to go back on tour, he went to the dentist, accompanied by his girlfriend, Ginger Alden, to have a cavity filled. He then returned to Graceland and drove through the gates for the last time. After a few hours of racquetball with his cousin Billy Smith, Elvis played

Above: Mennie Person met Elvis while he was browsing in a car lot on July 29, 1975. She told him that she liked his custom-made limo. The next day Elvis had one just like his delivered to her home.

Opposite page: Presley's constant struggle with his weight was a major aspect of his poor health. Before every tour he would go on a crash diet, during which he would lose as much as seventy pounds (32 kg) in a month.

the piano until nearly dawn. He and Ginger then retired. Instead of going to bed, however, Elvis grabbed a book, *The Scientific Search for the Face of Jesus,* and went into the bathroom. Several hours later, Ginger Alden woke up and noticed that Elvis was not there. She called out to him and when he failed to answer, she went looking for him. In the bathroom, she found him dead on the floor. Graceland immediately burst into chaos. Joe Esposito and Dr. Nichopoulos rushed to his side and immediately started administering CPR. Paramedics arrived and rushed Elvis to Baptist Hospital, where doctors frantically tried to revive him. All attempts at resuscitation failed, and Elvis Aron Presley was pronounced dead at 3:30 p.m. on August 16, 1977. The death was officially attributed to heart failure.

A small private funeral was held at Graceland on August 18. Reverend C. W. Bradley of the Woodland Church of Christ in Memphis officiated at the funeral. Comedian Jackie Kahane, who often appeared with Elvis in concert, gave the eulogy and Kathy Westmoreland, Jake Hess, James Blackwood, and the Stamps performed gospel songs. Elvis was buried in Forest Hills Ceme-

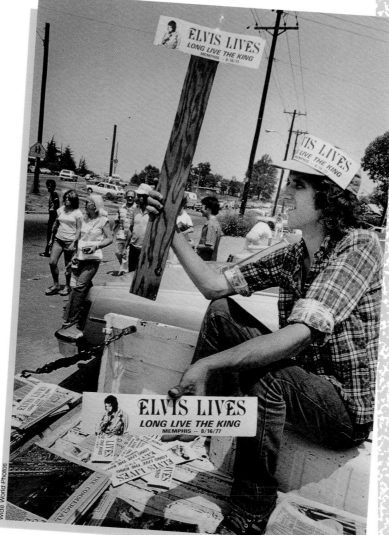

Wide World Photos

Wide World Photos

tery next to the grave of his mother. A few weeks later, however, there was an attempted body snatching. So on October 2, 1977, Vernon Presley had both Elvis and his mother moved to the meditation gardens in Graceland.

On January 16, 1971, six years before his death, Elvis Presley was named one of the Ten Outstanding Young Men of America by the United States Jaycees. It was the only award Elvis ever received in person, and he considered it one of his greatest accomplishments. After accepting the award from Jaycees President Gordon Thomas, Elvis spoke:

"...I learned very early in life that, without a song, the day would never end; without a song, a man ain't got a friend; without a song, the road would never bend; so I'll just keep singing the song...."

On August 16, 1977, when he was only forty-two, the song ended for Elvis Aron Presley.

Left: After his death, Memphis was besieged by thousands of grieving fans. Hustlers tried to take advantage of this grief by marketing a wide variety of Elvis paraphernalia and by starting rumors that he was actually still alive. Today, more than a decade after his death, Elvis Presley remains in the hearts and the minds of millions of fans around the world. Long live the King!

Opposite page: Fans from around the world have left written tributes to Elvis on the stone wall that surrounds Graceland. This photo was taken on August 16, 1986, nine years after the King's death.

chapter nine

ELVIS IS EVERYWHERE

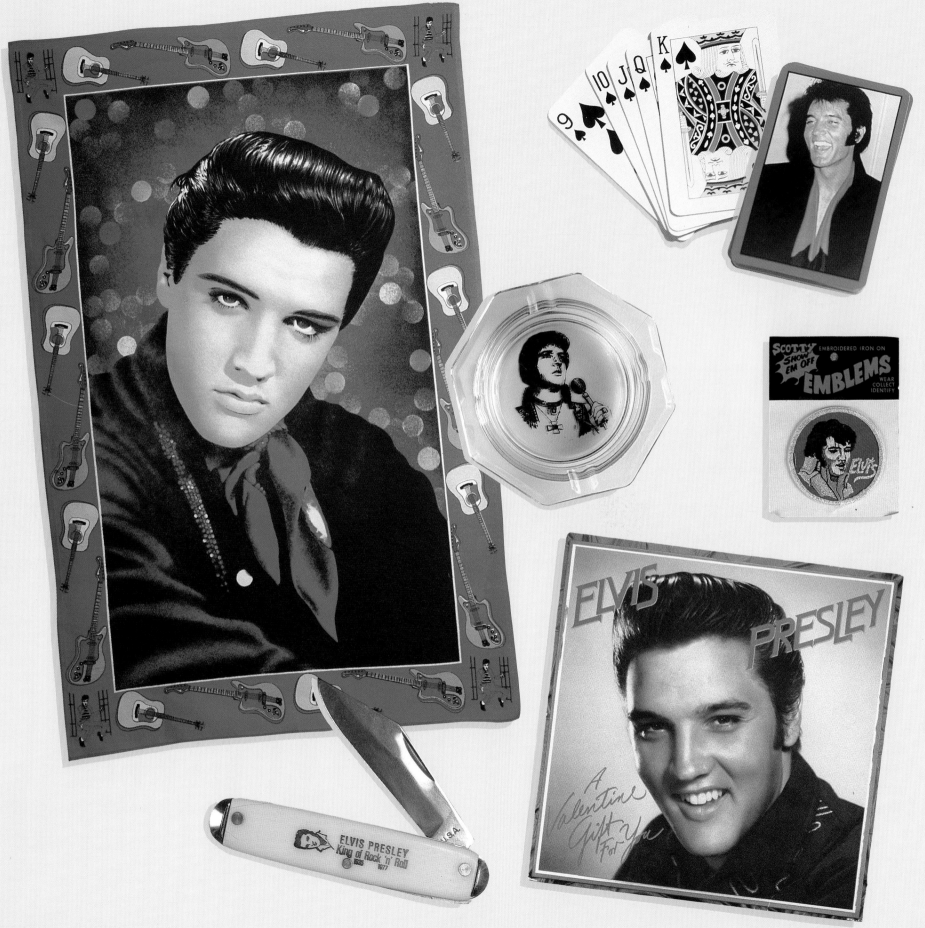

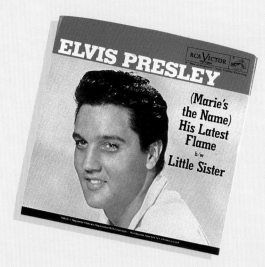

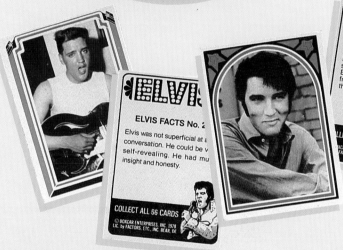

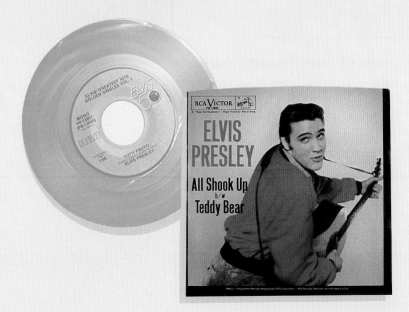

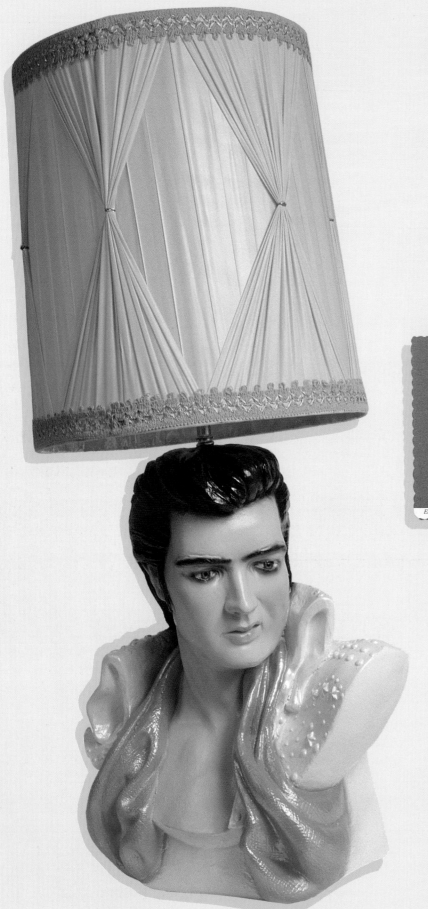

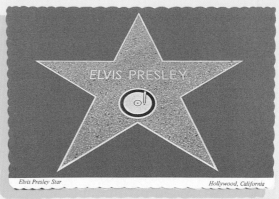

Elvis Presley Star   Hollywood, California

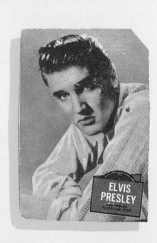

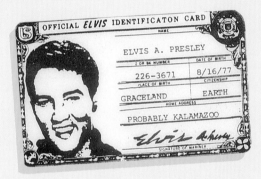

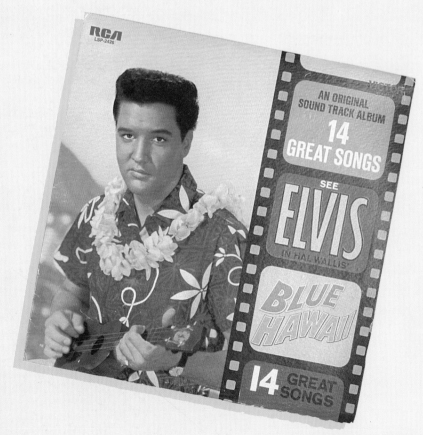

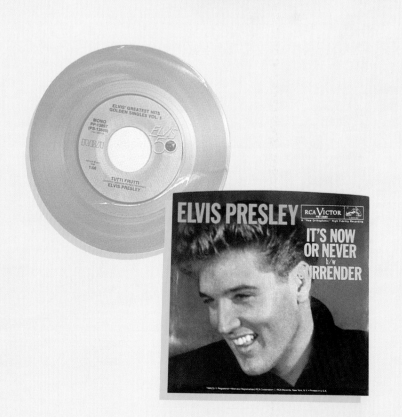

appendix i

TELEVISION

Louisiana Hayride
March 5, 1955; KWKH-TV.

Town and Country Jubilee
March 14, 1955; Interviewed by Jimmy Dean; WMAL,
Washington D.C.

Grand Prize Saturday Night Jamboree
March 19, 1955; KPRC-TV, Houston, TX.

The Roy Orbison Show
April 1, 1955; Odessa, TX.

Stage Show
January 28, 1956; Performed "Shake, Rattle, and
Roll" and "I Got a Woman;" NBC.

Stage Show
February 4, 1956; Performed "Baby, Let's Play House"
and "Tutti Frutti;" NBC.

Stage Show
February 11, 1956; Performed "Blue Suede Shoes"
and "Heartbreak Hotel;" NBC.

Stage Show
February 18, 1956; Performed "Tutti Frutti" and "I
Was the One;" NBC.

Stage Show
March 17, 1956: Performed "Blue Suede Shoes" and
"Heartbreak Hotel;" NBC.

Stage Show
March 24, 1956; Performed "Money Honey" and
"Heartbreak Hotel;" NBC.

The Milton Berle Show
April 3, 1956; Performed "Shake, Rattle, and Roll,"
"Heartbreak Hotel," and "Blue Suede Shoes;" CBS.

The Milton Berle Show
June 5, 1956; Performed "Hound Dog" and "I Want
You, I Need You, I Love You;" CBS.

Dance Party
June 20, 1956; KLAC-TV, Memphis, TN.

The Steve Allen Show
July 1, 1956; Performed "I Want You, I Need You, I
Love You" and "Hound Dog;" NBC.

Hy Gardner Calling
July 1, 1956; Interview following "The Steve Allen
Show" Performance; WRCA, New York.

The Ed Sullivan Show
September 9, 1956; Performed "Don't Be Cruel," "Love
Me Tender," "Ready Teddy," and "Hound Dog;" CBS.

The Ed Sullivan Show
October 28, 1956; Performed "Don't Be Cruel," "Love
Me Tender," "Love Me," and "Hound Dog;" CBS.

Holiday Hop
December 31, 1956; Interviewed by Wink Martindale;
KLAC-TV, Memphis, TN.

The Ed Sullivan Show
January 6, 1957; Performed "Hound Dog," "Love Me
Tender," "Heartbreak Hotel," "Don't Be Cruel," "Too
Much," "When My Blue Moon Turns to Gold Again,"
and "Peace in the Valley;" CBS.

APPEARANCES

American Bandstand

January 8, 1959; Telephone interview from West Germany; WFIL-TV, Philadelphia, PA.

Welcome Home Elvis

May 12, 1960; Performed "Fame and Fortune," "Stuck on You," and "Witchcraft/Love Me Tender" (in duet with Frank Sinatra;) ABC.

Elvis

December 3, 1968; Performed "Trouble"/"Guitar Man," "Lawdy Miss Clawdy," "Baby, What You Want Me to Do," "Heartbreak Hotel"/"Hound Dog"/"All Shook Up," "Can't Help Falling in Love," "Jailhouse Rock," "Love Me Tender," "Where Could I Go but to the Lord," "Up Above My Head," "Saved," "Blue Christmas," "One Night," "Memories," "Nothingville," "Big Boss Man," "Little Egypt," and "If I Can Dream"; Cut from the show were "Let Yourself Go," "It Hurts Me," "Blue Suede Shoes," "Don't Be Cruel," "That's All Right Mama," "Love Me," "When My Blue Moon Turns to Gold Again," "Tryin' to Get to You," and "Santa Claus is Back in Town;" NBC-TV.

Elvis: Aloha from Hawaii

January 14, 1973; Performed "Paradise, Hawaiian Style," "Also Sprach Zarathustra" (played by the Joe Guercio Orchestra), "See See Rider," "Burning Love," "Something," "You Gave Me a Mountain," "Steamroller Blues," "Early Morning Rain," "My Way," "Love Me," "Johnny B. Goode," "It's Over," "Blue Suede Shoes," "I'm So Lonesome I Could Cry," "I Can't Stop Loving You," "Hound Dog," "Blue Hawaii," "What Now My Love," "Fever," "Welcome to My World," "Suspicious Minds," "I'll Remember You," "Hawaiian Wedding Song," "Long Tall Sally"/"Whole Lotta Shakin' Goin' On," "Ku-u-i-po," "An American Trilogy," "A Big Hunk o' Love," and "Can't Help Falling in Love with You;" NBC-TV.

Elvis in Concert

October 3, 1977; Performed "Also Sprach Zarathustra" (played by The Joe Guercio Orchestra), "See See Rider," "That's All Right (Mama)," "Are You Lonesome Tonight?," "Teddy Bear"/"Don't Be Cruel," "You Gave Me a Mountain," "Jailhouse Rock," "How Great Thou Art," "I Really Want to Know," "Hurt," "Hound Dog," "My Way," "Early Morning Rain," and "Can't Help Falling in Love;" CBS-TV.

Elvis appears on "The Steve Allen Show."

Michael Ochs Archive

Love Me Tender

20 Century Fox, 1956. Running time: 89 minutes,
Filmed in Cinemascope.

CREDITS

Director	Robert D. Webb
Producer	David Weisbart
Screenplay	Robert Buckner
From a Story by	Maurice Geraghty
Director of Photography	Leo Tover
Editor	Hugh S. Fowler
Art Directors	Lyle R. Wheeler
	Maurice Ransford
Set Decoration	Walter M. Scott
	Fay Babcock
Costumes	Mary Mills
Assistant Director	Stanley Hough
Music	Lionel Newman
Orchestration	Edward B. Powell
Technical Advisor	Colonel Tom Parker

CAST

Vance Reno	Richard Egan
Cathy Reno	Debra Paget
Clint Reno	Elvis Presley
Mr. Siringo	Robert Middleton

Brett Reno . . . . William Campbell

Mike Gavin . . . . Neville Brand

Martha Reno . . . . Mildred Dunnock

Major Kincaid . . . . Bruce Bennett

Ray Reno . . . . James Drury

Ed Galt . . . . Russ Conway

Mr. Kelso . . . . Ken Clark

Mr. Davis . . . . Barry Coe

Pardee Fleming . . . . L.Q. Jones

Jethro . . . . Paul Burns

SONGS

"We're Gonna Move"

"Love Me Tender"

"Let Me"

"Poor Boy"

Loving You

Paramount, 1957, Running Time: 101 Minutes,
Filmed in VistaVision and Technicolor.

CREW

Director . . . . Hal Kanter

Producer . . . . Hal B. Wallis

Michael Ochs Archive

Screenplay . . . . Herbert Baker
Hal Kanter

From a Story by . . . . Mary Agnes

Director of Photography . . . . . Charles Lang, Jr.,
A.S.C.

Editor . . . . Howard Smith

Art Directors . . . . Hal Pereria
Albert Nozaki

Set Decoration . . . . Sam Comer
Ray Moyer

Costumes . . . . Edith Head

Assistant Director . . . . James
Rosenberger

Associate Producer . . . . Paul Nathan

Music Conducted &

Arranged by . . . . Walter Scharf

Vocal Accompaniment . . . . . . The Jordanaires

Technical Advisor . . . . Colonel Tom Parker

CAST

Deke Rivers (Jimmy

Tompkins) . . . . Elvis Presley

Glenda Markle . . . . Lizabeth Scott

Walter "Tex" Warner . . . . Wendall Corey

Susan Jessup . . . . Dolores Hart

Carl Meade . . . . James Gleason

Jim Tallman . . . . Ralphe Dumke

Skeeter . . . . Paul Smith

Wayne . . . . Ken Becker

Daisy Bricker . . . . Jana Lund

Harry Taylor . . . . Vernon Rich

Mr. Castle . . . . David Cameron

Mrs. Gunderson ....Grace Hayle

Mack ....Dick Ryan

SONGS

"Got a Lot o'Lovin' to Do"

"(Let's Have a) Party"

"(Let Me Be Your) Teddy Bear"

"Hot Dog"

"Lonesome Cowboy"

"Mean Woman Blues"

"Loving You"

King Creole

Paramount, 1958, Running Time: 116 minutes,
Filmed in Black & White.

CREDITS

Director ....Michael Curtiz

Producer ....Hal B. Wallis

Screenplay ....Herbert Baker

Michael Vincente

Gazzo

Based on the Novel ....*A Stone for Danny*

Fisher

by Harold Robbins

Director of Photography .....Russell Harlan,

A.S.C.

Editor ....Warren Low, A.C.E.

Art Directors ....Hal Pereira

Joseph MacMillan

Johnson

Set Decoration ....Sam Comer

Frank McKelvy

Costumes ....Edith Head

Assistant Director ....D. Michael Moore

Associate Producer ....Paul Nathan

Music Adapted and

Scored by ....Walter Scharf

Musical Numbers

Staged by ....Charles O'Curran

RENÉ CHATEAU presents

ELVIS PRESLEY

KING CREOLE

directed by
MICHAEL CURTIZ · HAL WALLIS
produced by

with CAROLYN JONES · WALTER MATTHAU · DOLORES HART · DEAN JAGGER · VIC MORROW

Vocal Accompaniment ......The Jordanaires
Technical Advisor..........Colonel Tom Parker

CAST

Danny Fisher..............Elvis Presley
Ronnie....................Carolyn Jones
Maxie Fields ....Walter Matthau
Nellie....................Dolores Hart
Mr. Fisher ....Dean Jagger
Forty Nina................Liliane Montevecchi
Shark....................Vic Morrow
Charlie LeGrand ....Paul Stewart
Mimi Fisher ....Jan Shepard
Sal ....Brian Hutton

SONGS

"Crawfish"
"Steadfast, Loyal and True"
"Lover Doll"
"Trouble "
"Dixieland Rock"

"Young Dreams"
"New Orleans"
"Hard Headed Woman"
"King Creole"
"Don't Ask Me Why"
"As Long as I Have You"

G.I. Blues

Paramount, 1960, Running Time: 104 minutes,
Filmed in Technicolor

CREDITS

Director ....Norman Taurog
Producer ....Hal B. Wallis
Screenplay................Edmund Beloin
Director of Photography .....Loyal Griggs, A.S.C.
Editor....................Warren Low, A.C.E.
Art Directors..............Hal Pereira
                            Walter Tyler

Set Decoration..............Sam Comer
                            Ray Moyer
Costumes ....Edith Head
Assistant Director..........D. Michael Moore
Associate Producer ....Paul Nathan
Music Scored &
Conducted by ....Joseph J. Lilley
Musical Numbers Staged
and Choreographed by......Charles O'Curran
Vocal Accompaniment ......The Jordanaires
Technical Advisor..........Colonel Tom Parker

CAST

Tulsa McLean ....Elvis Presley
Lili ....Juliet Prowse
Cookey ....Robert Ivers
Tina ....Leticia Roman
Rick ....James Douglas
Marla....................Sigrid Maier
Sergeant McGraw ....Arch Johnson
Jeeter ....Mickey Knox

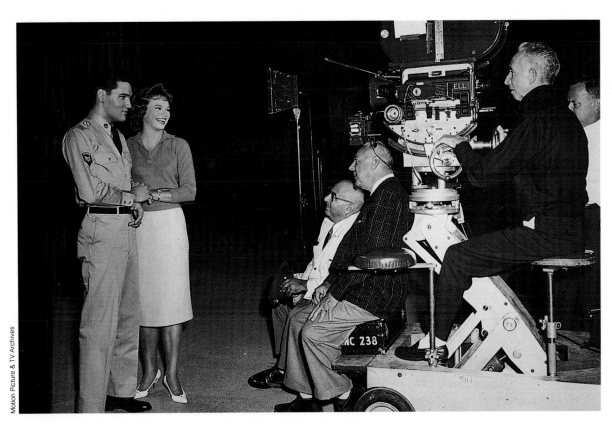

G.I. Blues

Captain Hobart	John Hudson
Mac	Ken Becker
Turk	Jeremy Slate
Warren	Beach Dickerson

SONGS

"What's She Really Like"

"G.I. Blues"

"Doin' the Best I Can"

"Blue Suede Shoes"

"Frankfort Special"

"Shoppin' Around"

"Tonight Is So Right for Love"

"Wooden Heart"

"Pocketful of Rainbows"

"Big Boots"

"Didja Ever"

Flaming Star

20th Century-Fox, 1960, Running Time: 101 minutes, Filmed in CinemaScope and DeLuxe Color.

CREDITS

Director	Don Siegel
Producer	David Weisbart
Screenplay	Clair Huffaker
	Nunnally Johnson
Based on a Novel by	Clair Huffaker
Director of Photography	Charles G. Clarke, A.S.C.
Editor	Hugh S. Fowler, A.C.E.
Art Directors	Duncan Cramer
	Walter M. Simonds
Set Decoration	Walter M. Scott
	Gustav Berntsen
Costumes	Adele Balken
Assistant Director	Joseph E. Rickards
Music	Cyril J. Mockridge
Music Conducted by	Lionel Newman

Orchestration	Edward B. Powell
Vocal Accompaniment	The Jordanaires
Technical Advisor	Colonel Tom Parker

CAST

Pacer Burton	Elvis Presley
Clint Burton	Steve Forrest
Roslyn Pierce	Barbara Eden
Neddy Burton	Dolores Del Rio
Sam Burton	John McIntire
Buffalo Horn	Rudolph Acosta
Dred Pierce	Karl Swenson
Doc Phillips	Ford Rainey
Angus Pierce	Richard Jaeckel
Dorothy Howard	Anne Benton
Tom Howard	L.Q. Jones
Will Howard	Douglas Dick
Jute	Tom Reese

SONGS

"Flaming Star"

"A Cane and a High Starched Collar"

Wild in the Country

20th Century-Fox, 1961, Running Time: 114 Minutes, Filmed in CinemaScope and DeLuxe Color.

CREDITS

Director	Philip Dunne
Producer	Jerry Wald
Screenplay	Clifford Odets
Based on a Novel by	J.R. Salamanca
Director of Photography	William C. Mellor, A.S.C.
Editor	Dorothy Spencer, A.C.E.
Art Directors	Jack Martin Smith
	Preston Ames
Set Decoration	Walter M. Scott
	Stuart A. Reiss
Costumes	Don Feld
Assistant Director	Joseph E. Rickards
Associate Producer	Peter Nelson
Music	Kenyon Hopkins
Orchestration	Edward B. Powell
Technical Advisor	Colonel Tom Parker

Flaming Star with Barbara Eden

Wide World Photos

Wild in the Country with Tuesday Weld

SONGS

"Wild in the Country"

"I Slipped, I Stumbled, I Fell"

"In My Way"

"Husky Dusky Day"

Blue Hawaii

Paramount, 1961, Running Time: 101 minutes, Filmed in Panavision and Technicolor

CREDITS

Director .Norman Taurog

Producer . . . . .Hal B. Wallis

Screenplay . . . . .Hal Kanter

Story . . . . .Allan Weiss

Director of Photography . . . . .Charles Lang, Jr.
A.S.C.

Editor .Terry Morse, A.C.E.

CAST

Glenn Tyler . . . . .Elvis Presley

Irene Sperry . . . . .Hope Lange

Noreen .Tuesday Weld

Betty Lee Parsons . . . . .Millie Perkins

Davis . . . . .Rafer Johnson

Phil Macy . . . . .John Ireland

Cliff Macy . . . . .Gary Lockwood

Rolfe Braxton . . . . .William Mims

Dr. Underwood . . . . .Raymond Greenleaf

Monica George . . . . .Christina Crawford

Flossie .Robin Raymond

Mrs. Parsons . . . . .Doreen Lang

Mr. Parsons . . . . .Charles Arnt

Sara . . . . .Ruby Goodwin

Willie Dace . . . . .Will Cory

Professor Joe B. Larson . . . . .Alan Napier

Judge Parker . . . . .Jason Robards, Sr.

Sam Tyler . . . . .Harry Shannon

Hank Tyler . . . . .Red West

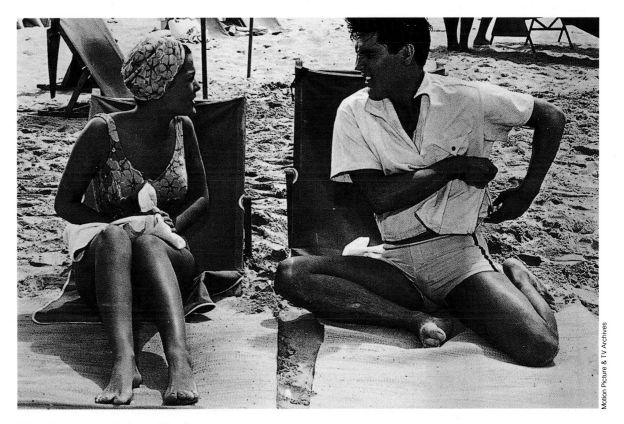

Motion Picture & TV Archives

Blue Hawaii with Joan Blackman

Motion Picture & TV Archives

Art Directors. . . . . .Hal Pereira
                                        Walter Tyler
Set Decoration. . . . . .Sam Comer
                                        Frank McKelvy
Costumes . . . . .Edith Head
Assistant Director . . . . .D. Michael Moore
Associate Producer . . . . .Paul Nathan
Music Conducted &
Scored by . . . . .Joseph J. Lilley
Vocal Accompaniment . . . . . .The Jordanaires
Musical Numbers
Staged by . . . . .Charles O'Curran
Technical Advisor. . . . . .Colonel Tom Parker

CAST

Chad Gates . . . . .Elvis Presley
Maile Duval . . . . .Joan Blackman
Sarah Lee Gates . . . . .Angela Lansbury
Miss Abigail Prentice . . . . . . .Nancy Walters
Fred Gates . . . . .Roland Winters
Jack Kelman. . . . . .John Archer
Mr. Chapman. . . . . .Howard McNear
Tucker Garvey . . . . .Steve Brodie
Enid Garvey. . . . . .Iris Adrian
Waihila . . . . .Hilo Hattie
Ellie Corbett. . . . . .Jennie Maxwell
Slena (Sandy) Emerson . . . . .Pamela Kirk
Patsy Simon. . . . . .Darlene Tompkins
Beverly Martin. . . . . .Christian Kay
Carl Tanami . . . . .Lani Kai
Ernie Gordon . . . . .Jose Devega
Ito O'Hara. . . . . .Frank Atienza
Wes Moto . . . . .Ralph (Tiki) Hanalei
Party Guest . . . . .Red West

SONGS

"Blue Hawaii"

"Almost Always True"

"Aloha Oe"

"No More"

"Can't Help Falling in Love"

"Rock-a-Hula Baby"

"Moonlight Swim"
"Ku-u-i-Po"
"Slicin' Sand"
"Hawaiian Sunset"
"Beach Boy Blues"
"Island of Blues"
"Island of Love"
"Hawaiian Wedding Song"

Follow That Dream

United Artists, 1962, Running Time: 110 Minutes, Filmed in Panavision and DeLuxe Color.

CREDITS

Director	Gordon Douglas
Producer	David Weisbart
Screenplay	Charles Lederer
Based on a Novel by	Richard Powell
Director of Photography	Leo Tover, A.S.C.
Editor	William B. Murphy, A.C.E.
Art Director	Mal Bert
Set Decoration	Fred McClean Gordon Gurnee
Costumes	Ruth Hancock
Assistant Director	Bert Chervin
Associate Producer	Herbert Mendelson
Music	Hans J. Salter
Technical Advisor	Colonel Tom Parker

CAST

Toby Kwimper	Elvis Presley
Pop Kwimper	Arthur O'Connell
Holly Jones	Anne Helm
Alicia Claypoole	Joanna Moore
H. Arthur King	Alan Hewitt
Mr. Endicott	Herbert Rudley
Nick	Simon Oakland
Carmine	Jack Kruschen
Teddy Bascombe	Robin Koon
Eddy Bascombe	Gavin Koon
Ariadne Pennington	Pam Ogles
George Binkley	Howard McNear
Judge Wardman	Roland Winters
Jack	Frank De Kova
Al	Robert Carricart
Blackie	John Duke
Governor	Harry Holcombe
Bank Guard	Red West

SONGS

"What a Wonderful Life"
"I'm Not the Marrying Kind"
"Sound Advice"
"On Top of Old Smokey"
"Follow that Dream"
"Angel"

Kid Galahad

United Artists, 1962, Running Time: 95 minutes, Color by DeLuxe

CREDITS

Director	Phil Karlson
Producer	David Weisbart
Screenplay	William Fay
From a Story by	Francis Wallace
Director of Photography	Burnett Guffey, A.S.C.
Editor	Stuart Gilmore, A.C.E.
Art Director	Cary O'Dell
Set Decoration	Edward G. Boyle
Costumes	Bert Henrikson Irene Caine
Assistant Director	Jerome Seigel
Production Supervisor	Allen Wood
Music	Jeff Alexander
Music Editor	Robert Tracy
Technical Advisor	Colonel Tom Parker

Kid Galahad

CAST

Walter Gulick	Elvis Presley
Willy Grogan	Gig Young
Dolly Fletcher	Lola Albright
Rose Grogan	Joan Blackman
Lew Nyack	Charles Bronson
Mr. Lieberman	Ned Glass
Mr. Maynard	Robert Emhardt
Otto Danzig	David Lewis
Joie Shakes	Michael Dante
Mr. Zimmerman	Judson Pratt
Mr. Sperling	George Mitchell
Marvin	Richard Devon
Ralphie	Jerry Morris
Father Higgins	Liam Redmond

SONGS

"King of the Whole Wide World"
"This is Living"
"Riding the Rainbow"
"Home is Where the Heart Is"
"I Got Lucky"
"A Whistling Tune"

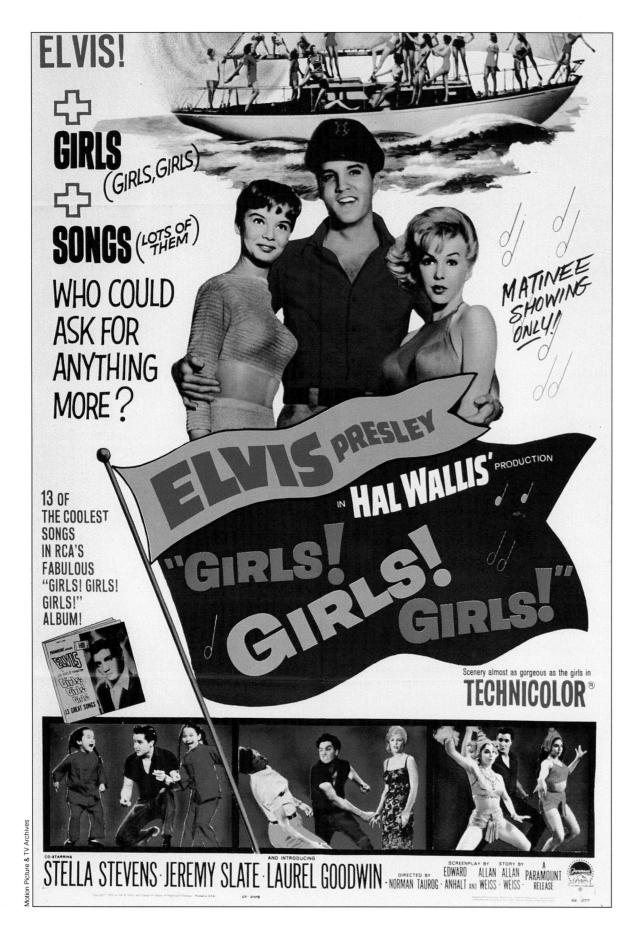

Girls! Girls! Girls!

Paramount, 1962, Running Time: 106 Minutes
Filmed in Panavision and Technicolor.

CREDITS

Director	Norman Taurog
Producer	Hal B. Wallis
Screenplay	Edward Anhalt
	Allan Weiss
Story	Allan Weiss
Director of Photography	Loyal Griggs, A.S.C.
Editor	Stanley Johnson, A.C.E.
Art Directors	Hal Periera
	Walter Tyler
Set Decoration	Sam Comer
	Frank R. McKelvy
Costumes	Edith Head
Assistant Director	D. Michael Moore
Associate Producer	Paul Nathan
Music Scored and Conducted by	Joseph J. Lilley
Musical Numbers Staged by	Charles O'Curran
Vocal Accompaniment	The Jordanaires
Technical Advisor	Colonel Tom Parker

CAST

Ross Carpenter	Elvis Presley
Robin Gantner	Stella Stevens
Wesley Johnson	Jeremy Slate
Laurel Dodge	Laurel Goodwin
Kin Yung	Benson Fong
Sam	Robert Strauss
Chen Yung	Guy Lee
Papa Stavros	Frank Puglia
Mama Stavros	Lily Valenty
Madam Yung	Beulah Quo
Mai Ling	Ginny Tiu
Tai Ling	Elizabeth Tiu
Bongo Player	Red West

Girls, Girls, Girls

SONGS

"Girls! Girls! Girls!"

"I Don't Wanna Be Tied"

"A Boy Like Me, a Girl Like You"

"Earth Boy"

"Return to Sender"

"Because of Love"

"Thanks to the Rolling Sea"

"Song of the Shrimp"

"The Walls have Ears"

"We're Coming in Loaded"

"Dainty Little Moonbeams"

It Happened at the World's Fair

Metro-Goldwyn-Mayer, 1963, Running Time:105 Minutes, Filmed in Panavision and Metrocolor.

CREDITS

Director	Norman Taurog
Producer	Ted Richmond
Screenplay	Si Rose
	Seaman Jacobs
Director of Photography	Joseph Ruttenberg, A.S.C.
Editor	Fredric Steinkamp, A.C.E.
Art Directors	George W. Davis
	Preston Ames
Set Decoration	Henry Grace
	Hugh Hunt
Assistant Director	Al Jennings
Music	Leith Stevens
Musical Numbers	
Staged by	Jack Baker
Vocal Accompaniment	The Jordanaires
	The Mello Men
Technical Advisor	Colonel Tom Parker

CAST

Mike Edwards	Elvis Presley
Diane Warren	Joan O'Brien
Danny Burke	Gary Lockwood
Sue-Lin	Vicky Tiu
Vince Bradley	H.M. Wynant
Miss Steuben	Edith Atwater
Barney Thatcher	Guy Raymond
Miss Ettinger	Dorothy Green
Walter Ling	Kam Tong
Dorothy Johnson	Yvonne Craig
Sheriff Garland	Russell Thorson
Boy Who Kicks Elvis	Kurt Russell
Fred	Red West

SONGS

"Beyond the Bend"

"Relax"

"Take Me to the Fair"

"They Remind Me Too Much of You"

"One Broken Heart for Sale"

"I'm Falling in Love Tonight"

"Cotton Candy Land"

"How Would You Like to Be"

"Happy Ending"

Fun in Acapulco

Paramount, 1963, Running Time: 97 Minutes, Color by Technicolor.

CREDITS

Director	Richard Thorpe
Producer	Hal B. Wallis
Screenplay	Allan Weiss
Director of Photography	Daniel Fapp, A.S.C.
Editor	Stanley Johnson, A.C.E.
Art Directors	Hal Periera
	Walter Tyler
Set Decoration	Sam Comer
	Robert Benton
Costumes	Edith Head
Assistant Director	D. Michael Moore
Associate Producer	Paul Nathan
Music Scored and Conducted by	Joseph J. Lilley
Musical Numbers	
Staged by	Charles O'Curran
Vocal Accompaniment	The Jordanaires
Technical Advisor	Colonel Tom Parker

Fun in Acapulco

Fun in Acapulco

CAST

Mike Windgren	Elvis Presley
Marguerita Dauphin	Ursula Andress
Dolores Gomez	Elsa Cardenas
Maximillian Dauphin	Paul Lukas
Raoul Almeido	Larry Domasin
Moreno	Alejandro Rey
Jose Garcia	Robert Carricart
Janie Harkins	Teri Hope
Mariachi Los Vaqueros	Mariachi Los Vaqueros
Mariachi Aquila	Mariachi Aquila
Dr. John Stevers	Howard McNear
Mr. Ramirez	Alberto Morin
Mrs. Stevers	Mary Treen
Poolside Guest	Red West

SONGS

"Fun Acapulco"

"Vino, Dinero y Amor"

"I Think I'm Gonna Like it Here"

"Mexico"

"El Toro"

"Marguerita"

"The Bullfighter Was a Lady"

"(There's) No Room to Rhumba in a Sports Car"

"Bossa Nova Baby"

"You Can't Say No in Acapulco"

"Guadalajara"

Kissin' Cousins

Metro-Goldwyn-Mayer, 1964, Running Time: 96 Minutes, Filmed in Panavision and Metrocolor.

CREDITS

Director	Gene Nelson
Producer	Sam Katzman
Screenplay	Gerald Drayson Adams
	Gene Nelson
From a Story by	Gerald Drayson Adams
Director of Photography	Ellis W. Carter, A.S.C.
Editor	Ben Lewis, A.C.E.
Art Directors	George W. Davis Eddie Imazu
Set Decoration	Henry Grace Budd S. Friend
Assistant Director	Eli Dunn
Music Conducted & Arranged by	Fred Karger
Musical Numbers Staged by	Hal Belfer
Technical Advisor	Colonel Tom Parker

CAST

Josh Morgan	Elvis Presley
Jodie Tatum	Elvis Presley
Papy Tatum	Arthur O'Connell
Ma Tatum	Glendall Farrell
Capt. Robert Jason Salbo	Jack Albertson
Selena Tatum	Pam Austin
Midge Riley	Cynthia Pepper
Azalea Tatum	Yvonne Craig
General Alvin Donford	Donald Woods
William George Bailey	Tommy Farrell
Trudy	Beverly Powers
Dixie Cate	Hortense Petra
Lorraine	Maureen Reagan
Mike	Joe Esposito

SONGS

"Kissin' Cousins"

"Smokey Mountain Boy"

"One Boy, Two Little Girls"

"Catchin' on Fast"

"Tender Feeling"

"Barefoot Ballad"

"Once Is Enough"

Motion Picture & TV Archives

Viva Las Vegas

Metro-Goldwyn-Mayer, 1964, Running time: 86 minutes, Filmed in Panavision and Metrocolor

CREDITS

Director .George Sidney
Producer .Jack Cummings
George Sidney
Screenplay . . . . .Sally Benson
Director of Photography . . . . .Joseph Biroc,
A.S.C.
Editor . . . . .John McSweeney,
Jr., A.C.E.
Art Directors . . . . .George W. Davis
Edward Carfagno
Set Decoration . . . . .Henry Grace
George Nelson
Costumes . . . . .Don Feld
Assistant Director . . . . .Milton Feldman

Viva Las Vegas with Ann-Margaret

Personality Photos, Inc.

Music . . . . .George Stoll
Musical Numbers
Staged by . . . . .David Winters
Technical Advisor . . . . .Colonel Tom Parker

CAST

Lucky Jackson . . . . .Elvis Presley
Rusty Martin . . . . .Ann-Margaret
Count Elmo Mancini . . . . .Cesare Danova
Mr. Martin . . . . .William Demarest
Shorty Farnsworth . . . . .Nickey Blair
Jack Carter . . . . .Jack Carter
Mr. Swanson . . . . .Robert B. Williams
Big Gus Olson . . . . .Bob Nash
Mr. Baker . . . . .Roy Engel
Showgirl . . . . .Teri Garr

SONGS

"Viva Las Vegas"
"The Yellow Rose of Texas"
"The Lady Loves Me"
"C'mon Everybody"
"Today, Tomorrow and Forever"
"What'd I Say"
"Santa Lucia"
"If You Think I Don't Love You"
"I Need Somebody to Lean On"

Roustabout

Paramount, 1964, Running time: 101 Minutes, Filmed Techniscope and Technicolor.

CREDITS

Director .John Rich
Producer . . . . .Hal B. Wallis
Screenplay . . . . .Anthony Lawrence
Allan Weiss
From a Story by . . . . .Allan Weiss
Director of Photography . . . . .Lucien Ballard,
A.S.C.

Art Directors . . . . .Hal Pereira
Walter Tyler
Set Decoration . . . . .Sam Comer
Robert Benton
Costumes . . . . .Edith Head
Assistant Director . . . . .D. Michael Moore
Associate Producer . . . . .Paul Nathan
Music Scored &
Conducted by . . . . .Joseph J. Lilley
Musical Numbers
Staged by . . . . .Earl Barton
Vocal Accompaniment . . . . . .The Jordanaires
Technical Advisor . . . . .Colonel Tom Parker

CAST

Charlie Rogers . . . . .Elvis Presley
Maggie Morgan . . . . .Barbara Stanwyck
Cathy Lean . . . . .Joan Freeman
Joe Lean . . . . .Leif Erickson
Madame Mijanou . . . . .Sue Ane Langdon
Harry Carver . . . . .Pat Buttram
Marge .Joan Staley
Arthur Nielson . . . . .Dabbs Greer
Freddie . . . . .Steve Brodie
Sam . . . . .Norman Grabowski
Lou . . . . .Jack Albertson
Hazel . . . . .Jane Dulo
Carnival Worker . . . . .Red West

SONGS

"Roustabout"
"Poison Ivy League"
"Wheels on My Heels"
"It's a Wonderful Life"
"It's Carnival Time"
"Carny Town"
"One Track Heart"
"Hard Knocks"
"Little Egypt"
"Big Love, Big Heartache"
"There's a Brand New Day on the Horizon"

Girl Happy

Metro-Goldwyn-Mayer, 1965, Running Time: 96 Minutes, Filmed in Panavision and Metrocolor.

CREDITS

Director .Boris Sagal
Producer . . . . .Joe Pasternak
Screenplay . . . . .Harvey Bullock
R.S. Allen
Director of Photography . . . . .Philip H. Lathrop, A.S.C.
Editor .Rita Roland, A.C.E.
Art Directors . . . . .George W. Davis
Addison Hehr
Set Decoration . . . . .Henry Grace
Hugh Hunt
Assistant Director . . . . .Jack Aldworth
Music .George Stoll
Vocal Accompaniment . . . . . .The Jordanaires
Technical Advisor . . . . .Colonel Tom Parker

CAST

Rusty Wells . . . . .Elvis Presley
Valerie Frank . . . . .Shelley Fabares
Mr. Frank . . . . .Harold Stone
Andy . . . . .Gary Crosby
Wilbur . . . . .Jody Baker
Sunny Daze . . . . .Nita Talbot
Deena Sheperd . . . . .Mary Ann Mobley
Romano . . . . .Fabrizio Mioni
Sergeant Benson . . . . .Jackie Coogan
Doc . . . . .Jimmy Hawkings
Brenwood Von Durgenfeld . . .Peter Brooks
Mr. Penchill . . . . .John Fielder
Besty .Chris Noel
Laurie . . . . .Lyn Edgington
Nancy .Gale Gilmore
Bobbie . . . . .Pamela Curran
Linda .Rusty Allen
Charlie . . . . .Dan Haggerty
Extra in Kit Kat Klub . . . . .Red West

SONGS

"Girl Happy"
"Spring Fever"
"Fort Lauderdale Chamber of Commerce"
"Startin' Tonight"
"Wolf Call"
"Do Not Disturb"
"Cross My Heart and Hope to Die"
"The Meanest Girl in Town"
"Do the Clam"
"Puppet on a String"
"I've Got to Find My Baby"

Personality Photos, Inc.

Girl Happy

Tickle Me

Allied Artists, 1965, Running time: 90 minutes, Filmed in Panavision and DeLuxe color.

CREDITS

Director .Norman Taurog
Producer . . . . .Ben Schwalb
Screenplay . . . . .Elwood Ulman
Edward Bernds
Director of Photography . . . . .Loyal Griggs
Editor .Archie Marshek
Art Directors . . . . .Hal Pereira
Arthur Lonergan
Set Decoration . . . . .Sam Comer
Arthur Krams
Assistant Director . . . . .Arthur Jacobson
Music Conducted &
Arranged by . . . . .Walter Scharf
Choreography . . . . .David Winters
Vocal Accompaniment . . . . . .The Jordanaires
Technical Advisor . . . . .Colonel Tom Parker

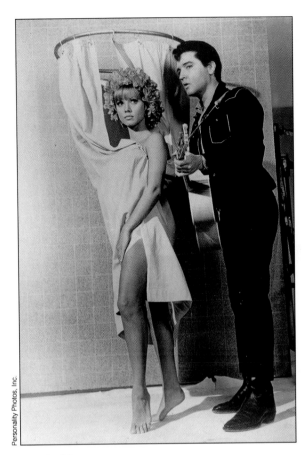

Tickle Me

CAST

Lonnie Beale	Elvis Presley
Vera Radford	Julie Adams
Pam Merritt	Jocelyn Lane
Stanley Potter	Jack Mullaney
Estelle Penfield	Merry Anders
Deputy Sheriff Sturdivant	Bill Williams
Brad Bentley	Edward Faulkner
Hilda	Connie Gilchrist
Barbara	Barbara Werle
Adolph	John Dennis
Mr. Dabney	Grady Sutton
Mabel	Allison Hayes
Ophelia	Inez Pedroza
Ronnie	Angela Greene
Henry	Robert Hoy
Janet	Laurie Burton
Clair Kinnamon	Linda Rogers
Bully in Bar	Red West

SONGS

"Long Lonely Highway"

"It Feels So Right"

"(Such an) Easy Question"

"Dirty, Dirty Feeling"

"Put the Blame on Me"

"I'm Yours"

"Night Rider"

"I Feel That I've Known You Forever"

"Slowly but Surely"

Harum Scarum

Metro-Goldwyn-Mayer, 1965, Running time: 95 minutes, Color by Metro Color.

CREDITS

Director	Gene Nelson
Producer	Sam Katzman
Screenplay	Gerald Drayson Adams
Director of Photography	Fred H. Jackman
Editor	Ben Lewis
Art Directors	George W. Davis H. McClure Capps
Set Decoration	Henry Grace Don Greenwood, Jr.
Assistant Director	Eddie Saeta
Music Conducted by	Fred Karger
Choreography	Earl Barton
Vocal Accompaniment	The Jordanaires
Technical Advisor	Colonel Tom Parker

CAST

Johnny Tyronne	Elvis Presley
Princess Shalimar	Mary Ann Mobley
Aishah	Fran Jefferies
Prince Dragna of Lunarkand	Michael Ansara
Zacha	Jay Novello
King Toransha	Philip Reed
Sinan	Theo Marcuse
Baba	Billy Barty
Mokar	Dirk Harvey
Julina	Jack Costanza
Captain Herat	Larry Chance
Leilah	Barbara Werle
Emerald	Brenda Benet
Sapphire	Gail Gilmore
Amethyst	Wilda Taylor
Assassin	Red West

SONGS

"Harem Holiday"

"My Desert Serenade"

"Go East, Young Man"

"Mirage"

"Kismet"

"Shake That Tambourine"

"Hey, Little Girl"

"Golden Coins"

"So Close, Yet So Far (from Paradise)"

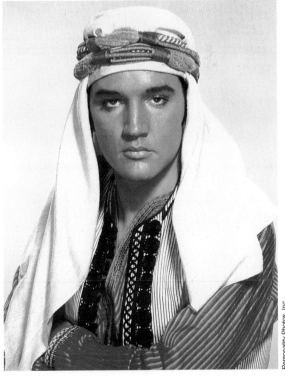

Harum Scarum

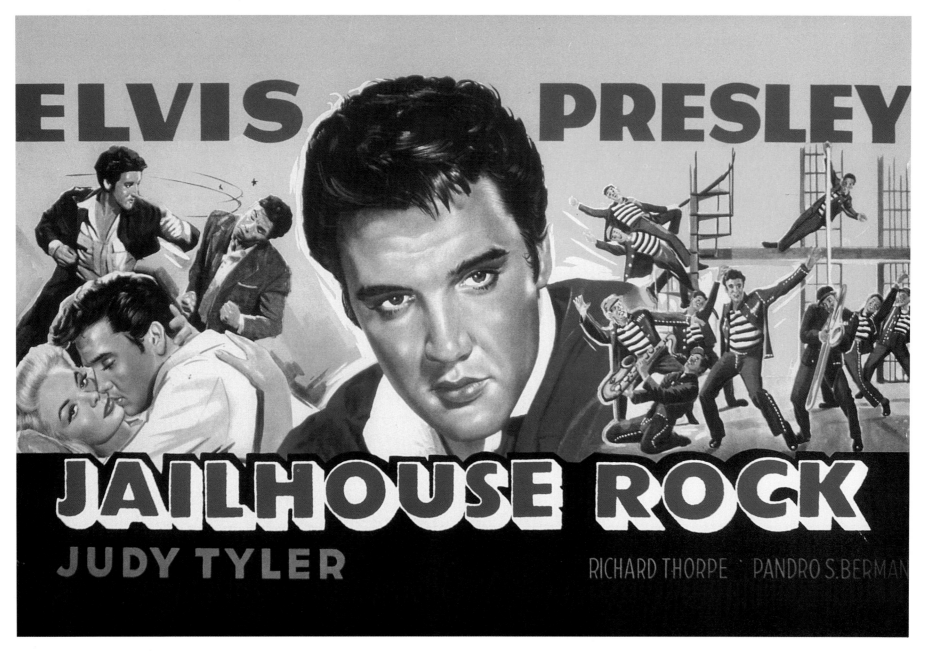

Jailhouse Rock

Metro-Goldwyn-Mayer, 1957, Running time: 96
Minutes, Filmed in CinemaScope.

CREDITS

Director	Richard Thorpe
Producer	Pandro S. Berman
Screenplay	Guy Trosper
Based on Story by	Ned Young
Director of Photography	Robert Bronner, A.S.C.
Editor	Ralph E. Winters

Art Directors	William A. Horning
	Randall Duell
Set Decoration	Henry Grace
	Keogh Gleason
Special Effects	A. Arnold Gillespie
Assistant Director	Robert E. Relyea
Associate Producer	Kathryn Hereford
Music Supervisor	Jeff Alexander
Songs Mostly by	Mike Stoller
	Jerry Leiber

Additional Songs by	Roy C. Bennett
	Aaron Schroeder
	Abner Silver
	Sid Tepper
	Ben Weisman
Technical Advisor	Colonel Tom Parker

CAST

Vince Everett	Elvis Presley
Peggy Van Alden	Judy Tyler

Hunk Houghton	Mickey Shaughnessy
Sherry Wilson	Jennifer Holden
Mr. Shores	Vaughn Taylor
Eddy Talbot	Dean Jones
Laury Jackson	Anne Neyland
Warden	Hugh Sanders
Sam Brewster	Percy Helton
Jack Lease	Peter Adams

SONGS

"Young and Beautiful"
"I Want to Be Free"
"Don't Leave Me Now"
"Treat Me Nice"
"Jailhouse Rock"
"(You're So Square) Baby, I Don't Care"
"Mystery Train"
"I Got a Woman"/"Amen"
"A Big Hunk O' Love"
"You Gave Me a Mountain"
"Lawdy Miss Clawdy"
"Can't Help Falling in Love"
"Memories"

Elvis on Tour

Metro-Goldwyn-Mayer, 1972, Running time: 93 minutes.

CREDITS

Directors	Pierre Adidge
	Robert Abel
Producers	Pierre Adidge
	Robert Abel
Director of Photography	Robert Thomas
Editor	Ken Zemke
Elvis's Wardrobe Designed by	Bill Belew
Associate Producer	Sidney Levin

Musicians	James Burton
	Charlie Hodge
	Ronnie Tutt
	Glen Hardin
	Jerry Scheff
	John Wilkinson
Conductor	Joe Guerico
Background Vocalists	Kathy Westmoreland
	The Sweet Inspirations
	J.D. Sumner and the Stamps
Comedian	Jackie Kahane
Writers for Mr. Kahane	Barry Adelman
	Barry Silver
Sound Supervisor	James E. Webb, Jr.
Music Recording	Carey Lindley
Rerecording Mixers	Lyle Burbridge
	William McCaughey
Technical Advisor	Colonel Tom Parker

SONGS

"Johnny B. Goode"
"See See Rider"
"Polk Salad Annie"
"Separate Ways"
"Proud Mary"
"Never Been to Spain"
"Burning Love"
"Don't Be Cruel"
"Ready Teddy"
"That's All Right (Mama)"
"Lead Me, Guide Me"
"Bosom of Abraham"
"Love Me Tender"
"Until It's Time for You to Go"
"Suspicious Minds"
"I, John"
"Bridge Over Troubled Water"
"Funny How the Time Slips Away"
"An American Trilogy"

Paradise Hawaiian Style

Paramount, 1966, Running time: 91 minutes, Color by Technicolor.

CREDITS

Director	D. Michael Moore
Producer	Hal B. Wallis
Screenplay	Allan Weiss
	Anthony Lawrence
From a Story by	Allan Weiss
Director of Photography	W. Wallace Kelley
Editor	Warren Low
Art Directors	Hal Pereira
	Walter Tyler
Set Decoration	Robert Benton
	Ray Moyer
Costumes	Edith Head
Assistant Director	James Rosenberger
Associate Producer	Paul Nathan
Music Conducted & Arranged by	Joseph J. Lilley
Musical Numbers Staged by	Jack Regas
Vocal Accompaniment	The Jordanaires
Technical Advisor	Colonel Tom Parker

CAST

Greg Richards	Elvis Presley
Judy Hudson (Friday)	Suzanna Leigh
Danny Kohana	James Shigeta
Jan Kohana	Donna Butterworth
Lani Kaimana	Marianna Hill
Pua	Irene Tsu
Lehua Kawena	Linda Wong
Joanna	Julie Parrish
Betty Kohana	Jan Shepard
Donald Beldon	John Doucette
Mr. Cubberson	Grady Sutton
Andy Lowell	Don Collier
Mrs. Daisy Barrington	Doris Packer
Moki Kaimana	Philip Ahn

Mrs. Belden	Mary Treen
Peggy Holdren	Gigi Verone
Dancer	Edy Williams
Rusty	Red West

SONGS

"Paradise, Hawaiian Style"

"Queenie Wahini's Papaya"

"Scratch My Back (Then I'll Scratch Yours)"

"Drums of the Islands"

"A Dog's Life"

"Datin' "

"House of Sand"

"Stop Where You Are"

"This is My Heaven"

Spinout

Metro-Goldwyn-Mayer, 1966, Running Time: 90 minutes, Filmed in Panavision and Metrocolor.

CREDITS

Director	Norman Taurog
Producer	Joe Pasternak
Screenplay	Theodore J. Flicker
	George Kirgo
Director of Photography	Daniel L. Fapp
Editor	Rita Roland
Art Directors	George W. Davis
	Edward Carfagno
Set Decoration	Henry Grace
	Hugh Hunt
Assistant Director	Claude Binyon, Jr.
Associate Producer	Hank Moonjean
Music	George Stoll
Musical Numbers	
Staged by	Jack Baker
Vocal Accompaniment	The Jordanaires
Technical Advisor	Colonel Tom Parker

Spinout

CAST

Mike McCoy	Elvis Presley
Cynthia Foxhugh	Shelley Fabares
Diana St. Clair	Diane McBain
Les	Deborah Walley
Susan	Dodie Marshall
Curly	Jack Mullaney
Lt. Tracy Richards	Will Hutchins
Philip Short	Warren Berlinger
Larry	Jimmy Hawkins
Howard Foxhugh	Carl Betz
Bernard Ranley	Cecil Kellaway
Violet Ranley	Una Merkel
Blodgett	Frederic Worlock

Harry	Dave Barry
Pit Crew	Red West
	Joe Esposito

SONGS

"Spinout"

"Stop, Look, and Listen"

"Adam and Evil"

"All That I Am"

"Never Say Yes"

"Am I Ready"

"Beach Shack"

"Smorgasbord"

"I'll Be Back"

Frankie and Johnny

United Artists, 1966, Running Time: 87 minutes, Color by Technicolor.

CREDITS

Director .Frederick De
Cordova
Producer . . . . .Edward Small
Screenplay . . . . .Alex Gottlieb
From a Story by . . . . .Nat Perrin
Director of Photography . . . . .Jacques Marquette
Editor . . . . .Grant Whylock
Art Director . . . . .Walter M. Simonds
Set Decoration . . . . .Morris Hoffman
Costumes . . . . .Gwenn Wakeling
Assistant Director . . . . .Herbert S. Greene

Associate Producer . . . . .Alex Gottlieb
Music Scored &
Conducted by . . . . .Fred Karger
Musical Numbers
Staged by . . . . .Earl Barton
Vocal Accompaniment . . . . . .The Jordanaires
Technical Advisor . . . . .Colonel Tom Parker

CAST

Johnny .Elvis Presley
Frankie . . . . .Donna Douglas
Cully . . . . .Harry Morgan
Mitzi . . . . .Sue Ane Langdon
Nellie Bly . . . . .Nancy Kovak
Peg . . . . .Audry Christie
Blackie . . . . .Robert Strauss

Clint Braden . . . . .Anthony Eisley
Abigail .Joyce Jameson
Joe Wilbur . . . . .Jerome Cowan

SONGS

"Come Along"
"Petunia, the Gardener's Daughter"
"Chesay"
"What Every Woman Lives For"
"Frankie and Johnny"
"Look Out, Broadway"
"Beginner's Luck"
"Down by the Riverside"
"Shout it Out"
"Hard Luck"
"Please Don't Stop Loving Me"
"Everybody Come Aboard"

Frankie and Johnny

Double Trouble

Metro-Goldwyn-Mayer, 1967, Running Time: 90 minutes, Filmed in Panavision and Metrocolor.

CREDITS

Director .Norman Taurog
Producer . . . . .Judd Bernard
Irwin Winkler
Screenplay . . . . .Jo Helms
Based on a Story by . . . . .Mark Brandel
Director of Photography . . . . .Daniel L. Fapp
Editor . . . . .John McSweeney
Art Directors . . . . .George W. Davis
Merril Pye
Set Decoration . . . . .Henry Grace
Hugh Hunt
Costumes . . . . .Don Feld
Assistant Director . . . . .Claude Binyon, Jr.
Music Score . . . . .Jeff Alexander
Technical Advisor . . . . .Colonel Tom Parker

CAST

Guy Lambert . . . . .Elvis Presley
Jill Conway . . . . .Annette Day
Gerald Waverly . . . . .John Williams
Claire Dunham . . . . .Yvonne Romain
Harry .Harry Weire
Herbert . . . . .Herbert Weire
Sylvester . . . . .Sylvester Weire
Archie Brown . . . . .Chips Rafferty
Arthur Babcock . . . . .Norman Rossington
Georgie . . . . .Monty Landis
Inspector de Groote . . . . .Leon Askin
Iceman . . . . .John Alderson
Captain Roach . . . . .Stanley Adams
Bit . . . . .George Klein

SONGS

"Baby, If You'll Give Me All Your Love"
"Could I Fall in Love"

"Long Legged Girls (With the Short Dress On)"
"City By Night"
"Old MacDonald"
"I Love Only One Girl"
"There Is So Much World to See"

Clambake

United Artists, 1967, Running Time: 97 Minutes,
Filmed in Techniscope and Technicolor.

CREDITS

Director . . . . .Arthur H. Nadel
Producers . . . . .Arnold Laven
Arthur Gardner
Jules Levy
Screenplay . . . . .Arthur Brown, Jr.
Story . . . . .Arthur Brown, Jr.

Director of Photography . . . . .William Margulies
Editor .Ernst R. Rolf
Art Director . . . . .Lloyd Papez
Set Decoration . . . . .James Redd
Assistant Director . . . . .Claude Binyon, Jr.
Associate Producer . . . . .Ernst R. Rolf
Music .Jeff Alexander
Choreographer . . . . .Alex Romero
Vocal Accompaniment . . . . . .The Jordanaires
Technical Advisor . . . . .Colonel Tom Parker

CAST

Scott Hayward . . . . .Elvis Presley
Dianne Carter . . . . .Shelley Fabares
Tom Wilson . . . . .Will Hutchins
James J. Jamison, III . . . . .Bill Bixby
Duster Hayward . . . . .James Gregory
Sam Burton . . . . .Gary Merrill
Sally . . . . .Suzie Kay
Ellie . . . . .Amanda Harley
Gloria .Angelique Petty
John
Gigi . . . . .Olga Kaya
Olive . . . . .Marlene Charles
Mr. Hathaway . . . . .Jack Good
Icecream Vender . . . . .Red West
Barber . . . . .Charlie Hodge
Bit . . . . .Joe Esposito

SONGS

"Clambake"
"Who Needs Money"
"A House That Has Everything"
"Confidence"
"You Don't Know Me"
"Hey, Hey, Hey"
"The Girl I Never Loved"

Double Trouble

Easy Come, Easy Go

Easy Come, Easy Go

Paramount, 1967, Running time: 95 minutes, Color by Technicolor

CREDITS

Director ....John Rich
Producer ....Hal B. Wallis
Screenplay.................Allan Weiss
Anthony Lawrence
Director of Photography .....William Margulies
Editor.......................Archie Marshek
Art Directors................Hal Pereira
Walter Tyler
Set Decoration..............Robert Benton
Arthur Krams
Costumes ....Edith Head
Assistant Director ....Robert Goodstein
Associate Producer ....Paul Nathan
Music Conducted &
Arranged by................Joseph J. Lilley
Technical Advisor..........Colonel Tom Parker

CAST

Ted Jackson ....Elvis Presley
Jo Symington...............Dodie Marshall
Dina Bishop ....Pat Priest
Judd Whitman..............Pat Harrington, Jr.
Gil Carey ....Skip Ward
Madame Neherina.........Elsa Lanchester
Captain Jack ....Frank McHugh
Lt. Marty Schwartz.........Sandy Kenyon
Cooper.....................Ed Griffith
Lt. Tompkins...............Reed Morgan
Lt. Whitehead ....Mickey Elley
Vicki.......................Elaine Beckett
Mary ....Shari Nims
Zoltan ....Diki Lerner
Tanya......................Kay York

SONGS

"Easy Come, Easy Go"
"The Love Machine"
"Yoga is as Yoga Does"
"You Gotta Stop"
"Sing, You Children"
"I'll Take Love"

Stay Away Joe

Metro-Goldwyn-Mayer, 1968, Running Time: 102 Minutes, Filmed in Panavision and Metrocolor.

CREDITS

Director ....Peter Tewksbury
Producer ....Douglas Laurence
Screenplay.................Michael A. Hoey
From a Novel by ....Dan Cushman
Director of Photography .....Fred Koenekamp
Editor......................George W. Brooks
Art Directors...............George W. Davis
Carl Anderson

Stay Away Joe

Set Decoration..............Henry Grace
                           Don Greenwood,
                           Jr.
Assistant Director..........Dale Hutchinson
Associate Producer........Michael A. Hoey
Music Scored by...........Jack Marshall
Vocal Accompaniment......The Jordanaires
Technical Advisor..........Colonel Tom Parker

CAST

Joe Lightcloud..............Elvis Presley
Charlie Lightcloud.........Burgess Meredith
Glenda Callahan..........Joan Blondell
Annie Lightcloud..........Katy Jurado
Chief Lightcloud...........Thomas Gomez
Hy Slager.................Henry Jones
Bronc Hoverty.............L.Q. Jones
Mamie Callahan..........Quentin Dean
Mrs. Hawkins..............Anne Seymour
Congressman Morrissey....Douglas Henderson
Lorne Hawkins............Angus Duncan
Frank Hawk...............Michael Lane
Mary Lightcloud...........Susan Trustman
Hike Bowers..............Warren Vanders
Bull Shortgun.............Buck Kartalian
Connie Shortgun..........Maurishka
Jackson He-Crow..........Sonny West
Orville Witt...............Michael Keller
Workman.................Joe Esposito

SONGS

"Stay Away, Joe"
"Lovely Mamie"
"Dominick"
"All I Needed Was the Rain"

Speedway

Metro-Goldwyn-Mayer, 1968, Running time: 94 minutes, Filmed in Panavision and Metrocolor.

CREDITS

Director...................Norman Taurog
Producer..................Douglas Laurence
Screenplay................Phillip Shuken
Director of Photography.....Joseph Ruttenberg
Editor....................Richard Farrell
Art Directors...............George W. Davis
                             Leroy Coleman
Set Decoration.............Henry Grace
                             Don Greenwood,
                             Jr.
Assistant Director..........Dale Hutchinson
Production Manager........G. Rex Bailey
Music.....................Jeff Alexander
Vocal Accompaniment......The Jordanaires
Technical Advisor..........Colonel Tom Parker

CAST

Steve Grayson..............Elvis Presley
Susan Jacks...............Nancy Sinatra

Speedway with Nancy Sinatra

Kenny Donford.............Bill Bixby
R.W. Hepworth............Gale Gordon
Abel Esterlake..............William Schallert
Ellie Esterlake.............Victoria Meyerink
Paul Dado..................Ross Hagen
Birdie Kebner..............Carl Ballantine
Juan Medala...............Poncie Ponce
The Cook..................Harry Hickox
Billie Joe..................Christopher West
Miss Charlotte
Speedway 100..............Miss Beverly Hills
Guitar Player...............Charlie Hodge
Stock-Car Racers..........Richard Petty
                             Buddy Baker
                             Cale Yarborough
                             Dick Hutcherson
                             Tiny Lund
                             G.C. Spencer
                             Roy Mayne

SONGS

"Speedway"
"Let Yourself Go"
"Your Time Hasn't Come Yet, Baby"
"He's Your Uncle, Not Your Dad"
"Who Are You? (Who Am I?)"
"There Ain't Nothing Like a Song"
"Your Groovy Self" (Sung by Nancy Sinatra)

Live a Little, Love a Little

Metro-Goldwyn-Mayer, 1968, Running time: 90 minutes, Filmed in Panavision and Metrocolor.

CREDITS

Director...................Norman Taurog
Producer..................Douglas Laurence
Screenplay................Michael A. Hoey
                             Dan Greenburg
Director of Photography.....Fred Koenekamp
Editor....................John McSweeney

Live a Little, Love a Little with Rudy Vallee

Art Directors	George W. Davis
	Preston Ames
Set Decoration	Henry Grace
	Don Greenwood, Jr.
Assistant Director	Al Shenberg
Production Manager	Lindsley Parsons, Jr.
Music Score	Billy Strange
Technical Advisor	Colonel Tom Parker

CAST

Greg Nolan	Elvis Presley
Bernice	Michele Carey
Mike Lansdown	Don Porter
Louis Penlow	Rudy Vallee
Harry	Dick Sargent
Milkman	Sterling Holloway
Ellen	Celeste Yarnall
Miss Selfridge	Mary Grover
Art Director	Micheal Keller
Newspaper Worker	Red West

SONGS

"Wonderful World"

"Edge of Reality"

"A Little Less Conversation"

"Almost in Love"

Charro!

National General Pictures, 1969, Running time: 98 minutes, Filmed in Panavision and Technicolor.

CREDITS

Director	Charles Marquis Warren
Executive Producer	Harry Caplan
Producer	Charles Marquis Warren
Screenplay	Charles Marquis Warren
From a Story by	Frederic Louis Fox
Director of Photography	Ellsworth Fredericks
Editor	Al Clark
Art Director	James Sullivan
Set Decoration	Charles Thompson
Costumes	Bob Fuca
	Violet B. Martin
Assistant Director	Dink Templeton

Charro!

Associate Producer ....Dink Templeton
Music Composed &
Conducted by ....Hugh Montenegro

CAST

Jess Wade ....Elvis Presley
Tracy Winters ....Ina Balin
Vince Hackett...............Victor French
Marcie ....Lynn Kellogg
Sara Ramsey ....Barbara Werle
Billy Roy Hackett ....Soloman Sturgess
Opie Keetch ....Paul Brinegar
Gunner ....James Sikking
Heff........................Harry Landers
Lt. Rivera ....Tony Young
Sheriff Dan Ramsey........James Almanzar
Mody ....Charles H. Gray
Lige ....Rodd Redwing
Martin Tilford ....Garry Walberg
Mexican ....Charlie Hodge

SONGS

"Charro!"

The Trouble With Girls

Metro-Goldwyn-Mayer, 1969, Running time: 97
minutes, Filmed in Panavision and Metrocolor.

CREDITS

Director ....Peter Tewksbury
Producer ....Lester Welch
Screenplay................Arnold Peyser
From a Story by ....Mauri Grashin
Based on a Novel by ....Day Keene
Director of Photography ....Jacques Marquette
Editor.....................George W. Brooks
Art Directors...............George W. Davis
                         Ed Carfagno
Set Decoration.............Henry Grace
                         Jack Mills

Costumes ....Bill Thomas
Assistant Director ....John Clark Bowman
Associate Producer ....William McCarthy
Choreography ....Jonathan Lucas
Music Score ....Billy Strange
Vocal Accompaniment ......The Jordanaires

CAST

Walter Hale ....Elvis Presley
Charlene..................Marlyn Mason
Betty......................Nicole Jaffe
Nita Bix ....Sheree North
Johnny ....Edward Andrews
Mr. Drewcoltl ....John Carradine
Mr. Morality ....Vincent Price
Carol Bix..................Anissa Jones
Maude ....Joyce Van Patten

Willy ....Pepe Brown
Harrison Wilby ....Dabney Coleman
Mayor Gilchrist............Bill Zuckert
Mr. Perper.................Pitt Herbert
Clarence ....Anthony Teague
Constable ....Med Flory
Deputy Sheriff.............Jerry Schilling
Gambler ....Joe Esposito

SONGS

"Swing Low, Sweet Chariot"
"The Wiffenpoof Song"
"Violet (Flower of NYU)"
"Clean Up Your Own Backyard"
"Sign of the Zodiac"
"Almost"

The Trouble with Girls

Change of Habit

Universal, 1969, Running time: 93 minutes.

CREDITS

Director	William Graham
Producer	Joe Connelly
Screenplay	James Lee
	S.S. Schweitzer
	Eric Bercovici
From a Story by	John Joseph
	Richard Morris
Director of Photography	Russell Metty
Editor	Douglas Stewart
Art Directors	Alexander Golitzen
	Frank Arrigo
Set Decoration	John McCarthy
	Ruby Levitt
Costumes	Helen Colvig
Assistant Director	Phil Bowles
Associate Producer	Irving Paley
Music	William Goldenberg

CAST

Dr. John Carpenter	Elvis Presley
Sister Michelle Gallagher	Mary Tyler Moore
Sister Irene Hawkins	Barbara McNair
Sister Barbara Bennett	Jane Elliot
Mother Joseph	Leora Dana
Lt. Moretti	Ed Asner
The Banker	Robert Emhardt
Father Gibbins	Regis Twomey
Rose	Doro Merande
Lily	Ruth McDevitt
Bishop Finley	Richard Carlson
Julio Hernandez	Nefti Millet
Desiree	Laura Figueroa
Amanda Parker	Lorena Kirk
Miss Parker	Virginia Vincent
Colom	David Renard
Hawk	Ji-Tu Cumbuka
Robbie	Bill Elliott
Mr. Hernandez	Rodolfo Hoyos

Personally Photos, Inc.

Change of Habit **with Mary Tyler Moore**

SONGS

"Change of Habit"

"Rubberneckin'"

"Have a Happy"

"Let Us Pray"

Elvis — That's The Way It Is

Metro-Goldwyn-Mayer, 1970, Running time: 97 minutes.

CREDITS

Director	Denis Sanders
Producer	Herbert F. Soklow
Director of Photography	Lusien Ballard
Editor	Henry Berman
Unit Production Manager	Dale Hutchinson
Assistant Director	John Wilson
Associate Film Editor	George Folsey, Jr.
Sound Recording	Larry Hadsell
	Lyle Burbridge
Elvis's Wardrobe Designed by	Bill Belew

Musicians	James Burton
	Glen Hardin
	Charlie Hodge
	Jerry Scheff
	Ronnie Tutt
	John Wilkinson
Background Vocalists	Millie Kirkham
	The Sweet Inspirations
	The Imperials
Conductor	Joe Guercio
Technical Advisor	Colonel Tom Parker

SONGS

"Mystery Train"

"Words"

"The Next Step Is Love"

"Polk Salad Annie"

"Crying Time"

"That's All Right (Mama)"

"Little Sister"

"What'd I Say"

"Stranger in the Crowd"

"How the Web Was Woven"

"I Just Can't Help Believin'"

"You Don't Have to Say You Love Me"

"Bridge Over Troubled Water"

"Words"

"You've Lost That Lovin' Feeling"

"Mary in the Morning"

"I've Lost You"

"Patch it Up"

"Love Me Tender"

"Sweet Caroline"

"Get Back"

"Heartbreak Hotel"

"One Night"

"Blue Suede Shoes"

"All Shook Up"

"Suspicious Minds"

"Can't Help Falling in Love"

FAN CLUBS

United States

Associates of Elvis Presley
    Fan Club
5320 534 D Ave. E #Q-47
Bradenton, FL 34203

Because of Elvis Fan Club
8880 Bellaire
Box 359
Houston, TX 77036

Elvis Arkansas-Style Fan Club
Beverly Rook
11300 Donnie Drive
Mabelvale, Arkansas 72103

Elvis Chicago Style
Mike Keating
Box 388554
Chicago, IL 60638

Elvis Country
Box 9113
Austin, TX 78766

Elvis Dixieland Fan Club
1306 Rosedale Drive
Demopolis, AL 36732

Elvis Echoes of Love
5930 Montibello
Imperial, Missouri 63052

Elvis Fan Club
Box 4537
Corpus Christi, TX 78469

Elvis Fans from Hoosierland
Sharon Ott
37 S. Lynhurst
Indianapolis, IN 46241

Elvis Fans United
110 Graston Avenue
Syracuse, NY 13219

Elvis Fever Fan Club
Anna Mae Meyers
4014 Keeners Road
Baltimore, MD 21220

Elvis Forever TCB Fan Club
Bob and Susan Still
Box 1066
Pinellas Park, FL 34665

Elvis and Friends
4017 Route 413
Levittown, PA 19056

Elvis Friends Are the Best
    Friendship Circle
Sandy Warehime
3007 Southpoet Avenue
Chesapeake, VA 23324

Elvis Friendship Circle
2908 Juen Lane
Bossier City, LA 71112

Elvis International Forum
Box 8383
Van Nuys, CA 91409

Elvis the King Fan Club
4714 Dundee Drive
Jacksonville, FL 32210

Elvis Lives On
13658 SE 192 St
Renton, WA 98058

Elvis Love's Burning
Box 7462
Shreveport, LA 71107

Elvis Memorial Club of Texas
Eddie Fadal
Box 3194
Waco, TX 76707

Elvis Memorial Fan Club of
    Hawaii
Charlie Ross
Box 15120
Honolulu, HA 96815

Elvis Memories
Box 2401
Livermore, CA 94550

Elvis Now
Sue McCasland
Box 6581
San Jose, CA 94550

The Elvis Presley Burning
    Love Fan Club
Bill DeNight
1904 Williamsburg Drive
Streamwood, IL 60103

E.P. Continentals
Box 1571
Kissimmee, FL 32741

The Elvis Presley Fan Club of
    the Capitol District
Lorraine Westervelt
Box 265
Schenectady, NY 12306

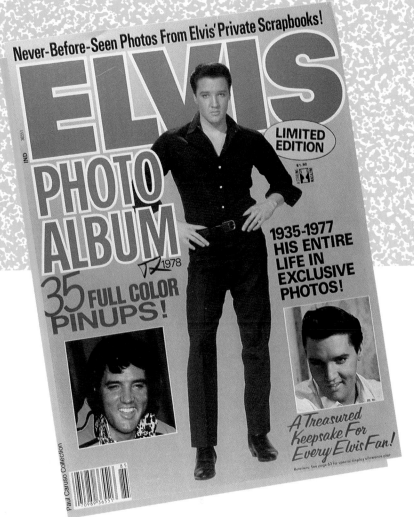

Graceland Express
Box 16508
Memphis, TN 38186

Having Fun with Elvis
Judy Dial
5310 Binz-Engleman Road
San Antonio, TX 78219

Elvis Presley Fan Club of
    Florida
John Beach
2202 Jammes Rd
Jacksonville, FL 32210

Elvis Presley Foundation
Box 1352
Norfolk, VI 23501

The Elvis Presley Foundation
    of New York
Alaine T. Silverman
130 Jerusalem Avenue,
    Apt. 321
Hempstead, NY 11550

Elvis Presley Memorial
    Society of Syracuse
Sue Fetcho
411 Mallard Drive
Camillus, NY 13031

The Elvis Presley TCB Fan
    Club of Chicago
Jeanne Kalweit
4939 Spring Road
Oak Lawn, IL 60453

The Elvis Special
Box 1457
Pacifica, CA 94044

The Elvis Teddy Bears
744 Caliente Drive
Brandon, FL 33511

Elvis That's the Way It Is Fan
    Club of Chicago
Carol Hopp
8730 S. Newland
Oak Lawn, IL 60453

Elvis, This One's for You
Casey Korenek
11400 February Drive
Austin, TX 78753

Elvis World
Bill Burk
Box 16792
Memphis, TN 38186

Elvis Worldwide Fan Club
Box 53
Romulus, MI 48174

Eternally Elvis TCB, Inc.
2251 N.W. 93rd Avenue
Pembroke Pines, FL 33024

For the Heart Fan Club
5004 Lyngail Drive
Huntsville, AL 35810

It's Only Love Elvis Presley
    Fan Club
Jack Myers
266 Harmony Grove Road
Lilburn, Georgia 30247

King of Our Hearts Elvis
    Presley Fan Club
Irene Maleti
2445 Fernwood Avenue
San Jose, CA 95128

Love 4 Elvis Fan Club
Fran Colvin
Box 2271
Clifton, NJ 07015

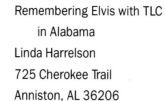

Memories of Elvis Express
Betty Roloson
302 Whitman Court
Glen Burnie, MD 21061

Mile High on Elvis Fan Club
Box 2332
Arvada, CO 80001

The New Jersey State
    Association for Elvis
Robert Job
304 Carlton Avenue
Piscataway , NJ 08854

Oklahoma Fans for Elvis
Keith Mitchell
302 S. 11th Street
Frederick, OK 73542

The Presley-ites Fan Club
Kathy Ferguson
6010 18th Street
Zephyrhills, FL 33540

The Presley Nation Fan Club
2941 Sunflower Circle East
Palm Springs, CA 92262

The Press'ley Press
Box 15230
Milwaukee, WI 53215

Reflections of Elvis
14210 Schwartz Road
Grabill, IN 46741

Remembering Elvis with TLC
    in Alabama
Linda Harrelson
725 Cherokee Trail
Anniston, AL 36206

Return to Sender
2501 Barclay Avenue
Portsmouth, VA 23702

Suspicious Minds Fan Club
Julie Banhart
4610 Owen
Memphis, TN 38122

TCB for Elvis Fans
Box 2655
Gastonia, NC 28053

TCB Elvis Presley Fan Club of
    Virginia
Box 1158
Glen Allen, VA 23060

TCB
Box 1925
Pittsfield, MS 01202

TCB Fan Club
2103 West 50th Street
Chicago, IL 60609

TCB in South Georgia
1220 N. Hutchinson Avenue
Adel, GA 31620

Then Now & Forever
Box 161130
Memphis, TN 38116

True Fans for Elvis Fan Club
Carole Brocher
Box 681
Saco, ME 04072

We Remember Elvis Fan Club
Pricilla Parker
1215 Tennessee Avenue
Pittsburgh, PA 15216

Welcome to Our Elvis World
Karen Oberender
5708 Van Dyke Road
Baltimore, MD 21206

Canada

Elvis in Canada
Fran Roberts
Box 6065
Station F
Hamilton
Ontario, Canada L9C 5S2

Elvis Presley King "O" Mania
    Fan Club
Mario Grenier
552 Croteau Quest
Thetford Mines, PQ
Canada G6G 6W7

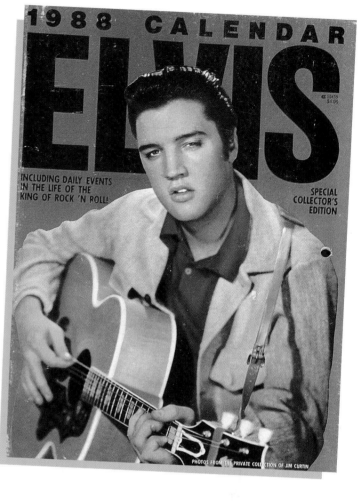

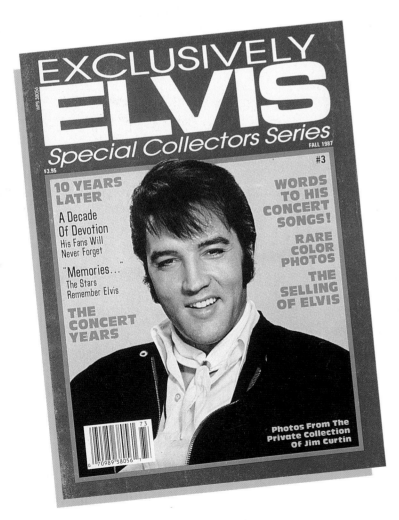

Elvis Till We Meet Again Fan
   Club
Doreen Oldroyd
124 Rankin Road
Sault Ste. Marie
Ontario, Canada P6A 4R8

England

The Elvis Collector
Earl Shilton
P.O. Box 10
Leicester, LE9 7FD
England

Elvis Is King Fan Club
David Trotter
59 Cambridge Road
New Silksworth
Sunderland SR3 2DQ
England

Elvis Today, Tomorrow &
   Forever Fan Club
Diana & Ray Hill
Box 41
Gloucester, GL1 2LN
England

Elvisly Yours
P.O. Box 315
London NW10
England

Leicester Branch of the
   Official Elvis Presley Fan
   Club
Box 4
Leicester
England

Europe

Elvis Presley Fan Club of
   Austria
Offenes Fach 543
A/1101 Wein,
Austria

International Elvis Presley
   Fan Club
Chaussee de Boendail,
   Brussels
Belgium

Elvis Presley Fan Club of
   Denmark
Bymuren 12
2650 Hvidoure
Denmark

Elvis Presley Sun Dial Fan
   Club
118 Rue De Lagney, 75020
Paris
France

Elvis Forever Fan Club of
   Greece
Adovsmani 3i
GR-16675, Glyfada
Greece

Dutch Elvis Presley Fan Club
H-1075 Budapest VII
Wesselenyiutca 16
Hungary

Elvis Presley Rock Fan Club
Via Brunamonti 2
62019, Recanati
Italy

Elvis Presley Fan Club of
   Luxembourg
25 Avenue Berchem
1231 Howald
Luxembourg

Elvis Presley Fan Club of
   Norway
Boks 52
1470 Lorenskog
Norway

Tidskriften Elvis
Box 3003
462 03
Vanersborg
Sweden

Elvis Presley Fan Club of
   Switzerland
Box 1678
2002 Neuchatel
Switzerland

Elvis Presley Gesellshaft
Post Fach 1264
D-8430 Neumarkt 1
West Germany

Australia

The Elvis Presley Fan Club of
   Queensland
Katrina Searle
PO Box 151
Chermside
Queensland 4032
Australia

Elvis Presley Fan Club of
   Tasmania
Elaine Green
PO Box 165
Sorrell 7172
Tasmania
Australia

Elvis Presley Fan Club
PO Box 82
Elsternwick
Victoria 3185
Australia

Japan

Elvis Presley Fan Club of
   Tokyo
PO Box 5
Kasai, Tokyo 134
Japan

Paul Caruso Collection

MILLION-SELL

* denotes those records that sold more than one million copies.

The releases in 1954 and 1955 were all from Sun Records. After 1955, all of Elvis Presley's records were released by RCA or RCA Victor.

The records are listed in order of release.

Michael Ochs Archive

1954

"That's All Right"...................................July 1954

"Blue Moon of Kentucky".........................July 1954

"Good Rockin' Tonight" ....September 1954

1955

"You're a Heartbreaker".........................January 1955

"Milkcow Blues Boogie".........................January 1955
                                        (Recorded in 1954)

"Baby, Let's Play House" ....April 1955

"I'm Left, You're Right, She's Gone" ....April 1955

"Mystery Train" ....August 1955

1956

"Heartbreak Hotel"* ....January 1956

"I Was the One"* ....January 1956

"I Want You, I Need You, I Love You"*..............May 1956

"Hound Dog"*....................................July 1956

"Don't Be Cruel"*...............................July 1956

"Blue Moon" ....September 1956
                                        (Recorded in 1954)

"Trying to Get to You"...........................September 1956
                                        (Recorded in 1954)

"Blue Suede Shoes"*............................September 1956

"Love Me Tender"*...............................October 1956

ING SINGLES

and Noteworthy Recordings

"Any Way You Want Me"* ....October 1956

"Paralyzed" ....September 1956
(Released on the EP
Elvis, Vol 1. Not
released as a single
until June 1983)

"Lawdy Miss Clawdy" ....September 1956

"Money Honey" ....September 1956

"Shake Rattle and Roll"........................September 1956

"When My Blue Moon Turns to Gold Again" ......September 1956
(Released on the EP
Elvis Vol 1. Not
Released as a single
until December 1986)

1957

"Too Much" ....January 1957
(Recorded in 1956)

"All Shook Up"* ....March 1957

"That's When Your Heartbreak Begins"* ....March 1957

"Teddy Bear"*..................................June 1957

"Loving You"* ....June 1957

"Jailhouse Rock"* ....September 1957

"(You're So Square) Baby, I Don't Care"...........September 1957

"Blueberry Hill" ....January 1957
(Never released as a
single. Originally
released on *Just For
You* EP.)

A ''New Orthophonic'' High Fidelity Recording

RCA VICTOR
47-6800

PLAYING FOR KEEPS
and
TOO MUCH

Paul Caruso Collection

"Mean Woman Blues" . . . . .October 1957

"Treat Me Nice"* . . . . .September 1957

"Peace in the Valley" . . . . .January 1957

1958

"Don't"* . . . . .January 1958

(Recorded in 1957)

"I Beg of You"* . . . . .January 1958

(Recorded in 1957)

"One Night"* . . . . .October 1958

(Recorded in 1957)

"Wear My Ring Around Your Neck"* . . . . .April 1958

"Hard Headed Woman"* . . . . .June 1958

"I Got Stung"* . . . . .October 1958

"Blue Christmas" . . . . .November 1957

"King Creole" . . . . .March 1958

(Never released as a
single. Originally
appeared on *King
Creole* soundtrack.)

Michael Ochs Archive

"Trouble" . . . . .March 1958

(Never released as a
single. Originally
appeared on *King
Creole* soundtrack.)

1959

Served in Army and did not record. A few singles recorded in 1958 were released
this year.

"A Fool Such As I"* . . . . .March 1959

"I Need Your Love Tonight" . . . . .March 1959

"My Wish Came True" . . . . .July 1959

"A Big Hunk o' Love"* . . . . .July 1959

1960

"Stuck on You"* . . . . .March 1960

"It's Now or Never"* . . . . .July 1960

"A Mess of Blues"* . . . . .July 1960

"Are You Lonesome Tonight"* .November 1960

"I Gotta Know"* . . . . .November 1960

"Fame and Fortune" . . . . .April 1960

"G.I. Blues" . . . . .April 1960

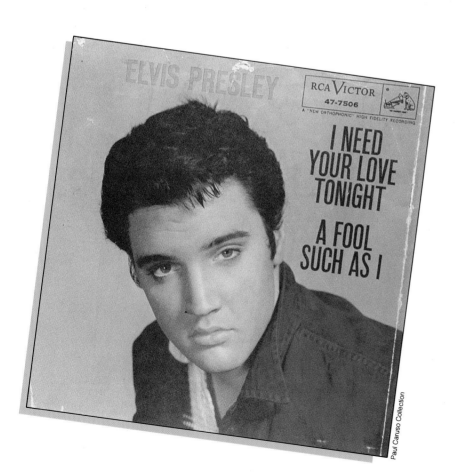

Paul Caruso Collection

1961

"Surrender"* ....February 1961

"I Feel So Bad"* ....May 1961

"Little Sister"* ....August 1961

"Can't Help Falling in Love"*....................December 1961

"Rock-a-Hula Baby"* ....December 1961

"Blue Hawaii"....................................(Never released as a single. Appeared on the *Blue Hawaii* soundtrack album, October 1961.)

"Follow that Dream" ....Released in 1961 on the *Follow That Dream* soundtrack album. Not released as a single until December 1986)

1962

"King of the Whole Wide World" ....May 1962

"Good Luck Charm" ....March 1962

"Anything That's Part of You"....................March 1962

"She's Not You"*..................................July 1962

"Return to Sender"* ....October 1962

"Where Do You Come From"*....................October 1962

1963

"One Broken Heart for Sale"*.....................February 1963

"(You're The) Devil in Disguise"*..................June 1963

"Please Don't Drag That String Around"..........June 1963

"Bossa Nova Baby"* ....October 1963

1964

"Kissin' Cousins"* ....January 1964 (Recorded in 1963)

"It Hurts Me" ....January 1964

"Viva Las Vegas"* ....April 1964 (Recorded in 1963)

"Suspicion" ....April 1964 (Recorded in 1962)

"What'd I Say" ....April 1964 (Recorded in 1963)

"Such a Night" ....July 1964 (Recorded in 1960)

"Ain't That Loving You Baby"*...................September 1964 (Recorded in 1960)

"Wooden Heart"* ....November 1964 (Recorded in 1960)

"Little Egypt" ....(Never released as a single. Released in October 1964 on the *Roustabout* soundtrack album.)

Michael Ochs Archive

Michael Ochs Archive

1965

"Crying in the Chapel"* ....April 1965
(Recorded in 1961)

"I'm Yours"* ....August 1965

1966

"Swing Low, Sweet Chariot".....................March 1966
(Recorded in 1960)

"Down in the Valley" ....(Never released as a
single. Appeared on
the *Spinout* soundtrack
album.)

"Spinout" ....September 1966

"If Every Day Was Like Christmas"...............November 1966

1967

"How Great Thou Art" ....April 1967
(Recorded in 1966)

"Long Legged Girl (with the Short Dress On)"......May 1967
(Recorded in 1966)

"Big Boss Man"..................................September 1967

"You Don't Know Me" ....September 1967

1968

"Guitar Man" ....January 1968
(Recorded in 1967)

"High Heel Sneakers"...........................January 1968
(Recorded in 1967)

"Let Yourself Go" ....June 1968
(Recorded in 1967)

"If I Can Dream"* ....November 1968

"Baby, What You Want Me to Do?" ....*Elvis—TV Special*

"Blue Christmas"................................*Elvis—TV Special*

"Can't Help Falling in Love"....................*Elvis—TV Special*

"Lawdy, Miss Clawdy"..........................*Elvis—TV Special*

"One Night" ....*Elvis—TV Special*

"Trouble/Guitar Man" ....*Elvis—TV Special*

"Where Could I Go But to the Lord?" ....*Elvis—TV Special*

(These songs were recorded for the Elvis television special. Most had been previously released in other recordings. The television recordings, however, are among the most vital Elvis ever made. Songs with release dates listed were singles.)

1969

"In the Ghetto"* ....April 1969

"His Hand in Mine" ....April 1969
(Released on the album
of the same name in
1960, but not released
as a single until 1969.)

"Suspicious Minds"* ....September 1969

"Don't Cry Daddy"*.............................November 1969

"Any Day Now" ....April 1969

"Long Black Limousine"..........................(Never released as a
single. Appeared on
From Elvis in Memphis
album.)

"Wearin' That Loved On Look"...................(Never released as a
single. Appeared on
From Elvis in Memphis
album.)

"Without Love (There Is Nothing)" ....(Never released as a
single. Appeared on
*From Memphis to
Vegas/From Vegas to
Memphis* album.)

"I'm Movin' On" ....(Never released as a
single. Appeared on
From Elvis in Memphis
album.)

1970

"The Wonder of You"*...........................May 1970

"Bridge Over Troubled Water" ....(Never released as a
single. Appeared on
That's the Way It Is.)

"Got My Mojo Workin'"..........................(Never released as a
single. Appeared on
Love Letters From Elvis.)

1971

"Kentucky Rain"* ....February 1971
(Recorded in 1969)

Michael Ochs Archive

"Amazing Grace" . . . . (Never released as a single. Appeared on *He Touched Me*.)

1972

"Bosom of Abraham" . . . . March 1972
(Recorded in 1971)

"He Touched Me" . . . . March 1972
(Recorded in 1971)

"An American Trilogy" . . . . April 1972

"Burning Love"* . . . . August 1972

(Both "An American Trilogy" and "Burning Love" were recorded live at Madison Square Garden. Studio versions were later recorded.)

1973

"Steamroller Blues" . . . . April 1973

1974

"I've Got a Thing About You Baby" . . . . January 1974
(Recorded in 1973)

"Promised Land" . . . . October 1974
(Recorded in 1973)

1975

"I Can Help" . . . . (Never released as a single. Appeared on *Elvis Today*.)

"Shake a Hand" . . . . (Never released as a single. Appeared on *Elvis Today*.)

1976

"Hurt" . . . . March 1976
"Moody Blue" . . . . December 1976
"She Thinks I Still Care" . . . . December 1976

1977

"Pledging My Love" . . . . July 1977
(Recorded in 1976)

"Way Down" . . . . June 1977
(Recorded in 1976)

1979

"Are You Sincere?" . . . . May 1979
(Recorded in 1973)

Michael Ochs Archive

The Elvis Reading List

Cocke, Marian J. *I Called Him Babe: Elvis Presley's Nurse Remembers.* Memphis State University Press, 1979.

Cogan, Arlene, with Charles Goodman. *Elvis, This One's For You.* Castle Books, 1985.

Dundy, Elaine. *Elvis and Gladys.* Macmillan, 1985.

Goldman, Albert. *Elvis.* McGraw-Hill, 1981.

Hammontree, Patsy. *Elvis Presley, A Bio-Bibliography.* Greenwood Press, 1985.

Harms, Valerie. *Tryin' to Get to You.* Atheneum, 1979.

Hopkins, Jerry. *Elvis: A Biography.* Simon and Schuster, 1971.

Hopkins, Jerry. *Elvis: The Final Years.* St. Martin's Press, 1980.

Jenkins, Mary, as told to Beth Pease. *Elvis the Way I Knew Him.* Riverpark, 1984.

Lacker, Marty, Patsy Lacker, and Leslie S. Smith. *Elvis: Portrait of a Friend.* Wimmer Brothers, 1979.

Lichter, Paul. *Elvis In Hollywood.* Simon and Schuster, 1975.

Mann, May. *Elvis, Why Won't They Leave You Alone?,* New American Library, 1982.

Marcus, Greil. *Mystery Train.* Dutton, 1975.

Marsh, Dave. *Elvis.* Rolling Stone Press, 1982.

Mathew-Walker, Robert. *Elvis Presley: A Study in Music.* Midas Books, 1979.

Nelson, Pete. *King! When Elvis Rocked the World.* Proteus, 1985.

Parker, Ed. *Inside Elvis.* Rampart House, 1978.

Pearlman, Jill. *Elvis for Beginners.* Unwin, 1986.

Presley, Dee, David Ricky, and Billy Stanley, with Martin Torgoff. *Elvis, We Love You Tender.* Delacorte, 1979.

Presley, Priscilla, with Sandra Harmon. *Elvis and Me.* Putnam's, 1985.

Presley, Vester, as told to Deda Bonura. *A Presley Speaks.* Wimmer Brothers, 1978.

Presley, Vester, and Nancy Rooks. *The Presley Family Cookbook.* Wimmer Brothers, 1980.

Rooks, Nancy, and Mae Gutter. *The Maid, the Man, and the Fans: Elvis Is the Man.* Vantage Press, 1984.

Shaver, Sean, and Hal Noland. *The Life of Elvis Presley.* Timur, 1979.

Stanley, Rick, with Michael K. Haynes. *The Touch of Two Kings.* T2K, Inc., 1986.

Staten, Vince. *The Real Elvis: Good Old Boy.* Media Ventures, Inc., 1978.

Stern, Jess. *Elvis: His Spiritual Journey.* Donning, 1982.

Umphred, Neal, ed. *Elvis Presley Record Price Guide.* O'Sullivan Woodside, 1985.

West, Red, Sonny West, and Dave Hebler, as told to Steve Dunleavy. *Elvis: What Happened?.* Ballantine, 1977.

Worth, Fred L., and Steve D. Tamerius. *All About Elvis.* Bantam, 1981.

Yancey, Becky, with Cliff Linedecker. *My Life With Elvis.* St. Martin's Press, 1977.

Additional Credits for Memorabilia

Page 126 (opener): Elvis clock courtesy, Little Rickie, NYC

Page 128: Pocket knife courtesy, Little Rickie, NYC; Elvis towel and playing cards, courtesy a private collection; ashtray, emblem, and albums, courtesy Lorraine Hansen collection

Page 129: Elvis hair button, courtesy Little Rickie, NYC; Elvis shrine photo, courtesy Amy Verdon; Elvis record and Elvis facts cards, courtesy Lorraine Hansen collection

Page 130: Elvis cologne, Elvis lamp, shroud of Elvis, courtesy Little Rickie, NYC; Elvis postcard and Elvis promotion card, courtesy Paul Caruso collection

Page 131: Church of Elvis magnet, courtesy Little Rickie, NYC; Elvis watch (left) and glass, courtesy a private collection; Elvis watch (right), courtesy Lorraine Hansen collection; albums and 45s, courtesy Lorraine Hansen collection

Page 132: Elvis I.D. card, courtesy Little Rickie, NYC; Elvis banner, courtesy a private collection; albums and 45's, courtesy Lorraine Hansen collection

Page 133: Elvis bust, courtesy Little Rickie, NYC; Elvis keychain, courtesy a private collection; Elvis money and Elvis cards, courtesy Lorraine Hansen collection

Page 134: Elvis apron and oven mitt, courtesy Little Rickie, NYC; Elvis salt and pepper, courtesy a private collection; Elvis card, albums, and 45's, courtesy Lorraine Hansen collection

Page 135: Graceland dirt, Elvis lighter, Presley family cookbook, courtesy Little Rickie, NYC; Elvis magnet and Elvis glass, courtesy a private collection

Index